NATE NASRALLA

LIVING
FORWARD
LOOKING
BACKWARD

*uncover more meaning in your
ordinary, everyday life*

LIVING FORWARD, LOOKING BACKWARD

To my beautiful wife: thank you for sticking with me,
entertaining my crazy ideas, and believing that
I can do anything. I love you.

Contents

Start Here

Are you living a meaningful life?

If we're honest, most of us will answer "not sure," or "not really." It's not an easy question to emphatically answer, "yes!" The reality is that our days are often filled with more routines than grand adventures, and we're not fulfilled by the common things in life. Eating cereal, sitting in traffic, and staying home on a Saturday when plans fall through won't make the headlines and highlights displayed on our social media feeds. Instead, we're captivated by the extraordinary things which will never happen within a normal week – getting a big promotion, finishing a marathon, buying a new car.

I believe, however, that your regular life is far more significant than you realize. There is deep meaning hiding in your everyday conversations and ordinary interactions – you just can't see it in the moment. You and I both need a framework to help us uncover more of the meaning in our ordinary, everyday lives. We need more stories.

We love stories, you see. It's how we're wired. Well-crafted stories stick with us. They allow us to recall life lessons in a memorable way. They also help us see the big picture during frustrating and disappointing circumstances. We even build our identities around stories. Where we came from, where we're going, the highs and lows – it's all part of the narratives we tell to the world.

When you begin to look at your life as one big story and recount your past, you'll discover that meaning often looks different from what we would have expected. Life's universal truths repeatedly show up in ways that feel strange to us. For example, it's easiest to hurt those we love most. The smallest steps achieve the biggest goals. Disappointing beginnings create happy endings. That all feels a little backward, right?

I noticed this after cycling through a rapid series of major life changes within a single year. After moving cities, merging companies, and getting married, all around the same time, I needed to process the change in a healthy way. Writing is therapeutic to me, so I began to create short stories from a series of notes I had jotted down during the preceding years. Whenever something special or notable stuck out to me, I opened the Notes app on my phone and I wrote down a quote I read, something a friend said over dinner, or a thought I had while jogging.

As I wrote and then connected these stories in a timeline, I noticed one consistent theme in every season of my life – paradox. A paradox is a feeling or experience that appears strange or backward in the moment, but it actually makes complete sense in the larger context.

I've come to believe our lives are shaped by these two principles: paradox and storytelling. You'll see it's true when you look back on your own life's events in one, overarching story. You'll discover there is a greater, unseen purpose behind it all, even when your circumstances don't feel significant. When life doesn't make sense, it's because the plotline is still unfolding in ways you don't expect. I wrote this book to help you see how these two principles are at work in your life.

Now, the great thing about stories is they're universal – you have a life story, as does everyone else. And because every story ever written contains conflict, we know that we'll all encounter conflict at some point in our lives. Sooner or later, we find ourselves facing a crossroads, difficult decisions, or relational strain. In these moments of tension, we don't often understand the long-term significance of what's developing. We rarely value the experience as we live it. It's only after making it to the other side of conflict that we can look back, find meaning, and apply a new lesson to our lives as we keep on living forward.

While I've watched friends navigate conflicts that happen *to* them – illness, death, unexpected tragedies – my greatest struggles seem to rise up from *within* me – anxiety, fear, loneliness. Conflict in my story has felt like friendly-fire. Something that's unexpected, bewildering, and it leaves you uncertain about how to fight back.

As you continue to read, you'll see that my story's conflicts continually leave me saying, "This again?" I face the battles I thought I had already fought (and won) time and time again. It's demoralizing to feel like I'm always re-fighting the same battles. Nonetheless, I've never kept a daily journal nor committed much time to reflect on my life, so I often repeat the errors from which I should have already learned. As you read on, my hope is that you learn from these mistakes.

More importantly, my hope is that you discover how these two concepts, the framework of storytelling and the principle of paradox, will help you uncover more meaning in the ordinary, everyday moments of your own life.

If you come from a faith-based worldview, you'll notice that these two elements consistently and coherently align with the Christian worldview. If you don't come from any faith-based worldview, keep reading. Understanding these elements will help you discover greater meaning in your everyday life too, regardless of your religious beliefs.

Costa Rican Watermelons

June 2013

- slow down and you'll see more in life -

I didn't know that we'd end up there. It just sort of happened. So ultimately, after deciding to slow down, I was actually seeing more of the country and absorbing more of our trip.

The majority of my days feel like plain vanilla ice cream. Unremarkable and predictable. I eat, get dressed, commute, and spend time transitioning from one routine to another. Can you relate? It would seem, then, that breaking from my daily schedule to backpack Latin America for weeks with a good friend would have produced all kinds of new learning and maturity. In reality, the excess of new experiences and photogenic moments distracted me from an important reality. I missed the fact that we don't need exotic trips to learn from life. We just need to look around. I found that when I finally stopped hurrying from one adventure to the next, I began to grow. I actually saw more of the country by slowing down.

"Dude. This. Sucks," Greg said as he lay out on the hard tile floor at the Ft. Lauderdale airport. He rolled over as I nodded in agreement. I glanced at my watch. It was about 1:00 a.m. We had been lying on the ground for three hours thanks to a flight delay, and we weren't interested in experimenting with the only restaurant in the terminal. It served warm beer and "Chicago" style hot dogs from rotating warming trays.

"Yeah… not quite the start we were hoping for," I laughed half-heartedly.

I was too tired to laugh, but I had to feign some excitement like it was all just a part of the adventure. Greg and I had $4,000 in traveling money between us, and we'd decided to travel to Nicaragua and Costa Rica for one month before we each started new jobs. I had been hired to work for a consulting firm in Chicago. Greg was headed off to work for a big energy company in Philadelphia. It seemed appropriate that a new adventure would precede new cities, new jobs, and new paychecks.

Here's a travel tip for you. If you're planning to travel with only $2,000 to your name, you need to start with a fair amount of confidence that you won't run out of money along the way. So, to save for food and hostels, Greg and I decided we'd book our flights to Managua, Nicaragua on some budget airline known for canceling or changing flights without warning.

Clearly, our idea wasn't as smart as it first sounded.

I reached into my backpack and grabbed a small folder of papers. "We planned this trip down a T, but I guess that doesn't mean we'll get to follow the plan," I said to Greg. I realized then that backpacking requires an odd blend of meticulousness when planning a route, but spontaneity to actually travel it.

"Now boarding: All passengers to Managua. Please, line up near the gate."

"Thank heavens. Let's go, Greg."

Once aboard our plane, I settled into my seat and slipped my sandals off my feet. I stretched out to the whopping 20" of legroom that tin-can-of-an-airplane allowed, and I closed my eyes. I wondered if we'd encounter more setbacks once we landed in Nicaragua, or if we'd have a smoother trip from that point forward. The engines spooled up and the pilot taxied out to the runway through the humid summer air. I created future Instagram captions in my head while drifting off to sleep, "Here we are diving into an active volcano to catch alligators..."

———

"So, man, what do you wanna do?"

Greg set his phone on his chest and lifted his head from his pillow, awaiting my response. We had done a lot of traveling already, and we had generally stuck to our plan. We checked off cities and experiences from our list, one after the other. We actually did climb an active volcano (sadly, there were no alligators), surfed next to small sharks, and watched the sun set over the ocean while eating tacos from a little lady grilling on a roadside cart. By all standards, we had moved from one extraordinary adventure to another. Even traveling from city to city was interesting. We'd throw our backpacks atop a 10-passenger van and cruise the narrow streets, taking it all in.

Despite it all, I had grown restless.

Sitting on our hostel beds, I found myself looking for the next big thing. I didn't feel full. I just wanted to do, see, and explore more. I felt like our trip, if not built on one bold moment after another, wouldn't be that epic pre-wife-and-kids trip you recall with a longing fondness as you try to calm a baby that's crying and pooping at 3 a.m.

"I'm not sure man, but I know I want to do something. Why don't we just go outside? We can walk around until we find something. Or at least until something finds us."

I framed it as a suggestion, but before Greg could reply, I had already put on my sandals and sat at the edge of my bed. I was halfway to the door by the time Greg shrugged his shoulders as if to say, "Sure man, whatever you want."

He would have given me the same shrug regardless. That's Greg. He was the ultimate travel companion. Up for whatever and content with anything from playing games on his cell phone to jumping off the tallest bungee platform in Latin America (which we also did). If I was honest with myself, I'd have admitted I envied Greg's ability to enjoy our ordinary moments just as much as the high-octane ones. It was clear Greg's ease would sustain him after our trip, continuing in his everyday life at work and home.

I wanted that inner calm.

Throughout our trip, Greg's needs were pretty modest. He focused on two things; finding one good bottle of wine and ensuring we had enough capital left in our bank accounts to buy it. That's all he cared about. My mind, on the other hand, was an unquenchable firestorm. As soon as we finished one activity, I was already burning for the next and figuring out the fastest way to get there. Instead of relishing the high of a new experience, I was over that event, past its memory, and yearning for something different.

Greg slapped on some sandals and pulled on a yellow tank top he'd bought for $1 on the beach. Then, we left the hostel to cure my restlessness. We wandered down the county road for 15 minutes before Greg finally asked, "Where are we going?"

We had drifted by the fire station, the local park, a grocery store, and we'd pretty much covered everything our little Costa Rican mountain town offered. "To that corner store," I pointed straight ahead. "I'm thirsty. You want something? Maybe they have ice cream."

We hadn't found anything to do, but I figured I'd drive Greg nuts if we just kept wandering around until we stumbled across something unique enough to satiate my hunger for adventure. I stepped into the little store and scanned the rows of snacks. I saw a little woman sitting behind the counter, quietly counting coins and ignoring us as we stepped inside.

"Hola," I said as I walked toward a standing refrigerator. I eased the glass door open and tossed Greg a frosty bottle of Coca-Cola.

"We're looking for something to do. Is there anything you recommend?" I asked her in Spanish.

Have you ever seen the movie *Pirates of the Caribbean?* Where the pirates become part of the ship's mast and railings after living at sea for so long? It was the same deal with this woman. I guessed she had been sitting on that same stool since she was a teenager, restocking rows of chips for decades. I assumed that after her years of shop-tending and coin-counting, she'd know more about the town than Google and a guidebook combined.

I leveraged my Spanish to learn that not far up the road, while the tourists paid $90 to relax in fancy hot springs fed by the Arenal volcano, the locals had their own hangout in the same thermal streams. The shop tender said that if we journeyed up the hillside for a half-mile to a wooded entrance hidden on the side of the county road and passed a few low-hanging trees, there would be a clearing that opened into a set of naturally formed rock baths (simple directions, right?). Each cascaded into the next, all fed by the volcano's heat, creating a hideaway for the city's Ticos (a.k.a. locals) to enjoy.

She told that us that with some "sandias y cervezas" – watermelons and beer – we'd make fast friends. I relayed the good news to Greg, who speaks Portuguese but not Spanish, and I saw him flash a smile. I paid for our supplies and with some extra direction from the woman, we learned how to direct a taxi to the right spot along the highway.

It was almost sundown as we stepped back onto the street, so we decided to head straight to the rock baths. Greg whispered as we walked, "I wonder what other secrets that lady's hiding behind her counter."

———

"Want beer?" I asked in Spanish, holding up a few cans above the steam and passing them to our neighbors sitting in a pool of thermal water.

"This is pretty wild, dude. Who would have guessed there's a rainforest paradise hanging out behind some trees on the side of a random highway?" Greg said while slamming a watermelon on a pointed rock.

He stuck a spoon in my half of the watermelon and passed it to me. "Yeah man. It's amazing. Refreshing, too. Too bad it's so dark now. I can't even take a picture," I lamented.

"Maybe that's part of the beauty," Greg said. "I mean, we just have to enjoy it in the moment, you know? It's one of those things we'll get to remember in our heads."

I sank down and dipped my head below the water. Bubbles leaked from my nose as they escaped back to the surface. I thought about Greg's words after drowning out the sounds around me. We had completed most of our journey at this point, but I was just beginning to realize that in my quest to create an extraordinary trek – documenting each step with photos and videos and searching for one high after another – I had been trading joy in the present for thrills in the future. I cared more about recounting impressive past stories than savoring them as I lived them with a beloved friend.

I obsessed over finding new highs, and I had overlooked the wonder all around me. I breezed past the simple beauty in spending time with one of my best friends. I robbed myself of the bliss found in just looking around. I was always searching for the "next big thing."

We stumbled into an incredible memory of Costa Rican hot springs and watermelons because two people were living their ordinary, everyday lives. Had we not wandered into that store and met the woman who'd sat behind its counter for years, we'd never have discovered such a picturesque, local secret. If not for the taxi driver who'd driven the same roads for years, we may never have found the hot springs along the highway's curves.

"I think it's good not to have expectations. Just to feel what we feel and find what we find," I said to Greg after emerging from the water, sharing what I'd discovered below the surface.

"Yep, I totally agree," Greg said, closing his eyes and laying back.

I continued, "I don't think I'm very good at slowing down. I don't really soak up what's happening around me. You know? Like, I need to look at all the good our life is so full of. I think I'm supposed to be learning that."

"I also agree with that," Greg laughed as he listened to me uncover what he'd known all along.

We sat in those baths eating watermelons and drinking beer for a good while longer, appreciating the moments for what they were instead of how they compared to our expectations. The longer we sat, the more content I felt. The longer I absorbed the conversations around me, the less interested I became in moving on to the next activity. I was no longer sitting in suspense of the trip's next step. I felt free from the weight of my mental expectations. Ultimately, I was in fact seeing more of the country after deciding to slow down.

There are two battles fought on opposite fronts that block us from noticing the natural wonder in our lives. The first and more prominent battle for me is a hyper-focus on success. I forget to slow down and squeeze the learning out of my life's current season because I'm too focused on catching the next shiny object. I don't sit still, and I miss the small miracles of life as a result. I wake up demanding something new from the world each morning, forgetting that simply waking up is a gift.

Chasing success may get us to the pinnacle in one season of life, but it leaves us searching for something more in the next. Conquest sounds big and meaningful, but the idea that increasing accomplishment can fulfill our deepest longings is a slippery temptation with no end in sight. Personally, my demands for instant gratification and my impatience for success too often disrupt the maturity that's gained through steadily pursuing a long-term goal.

The second and opposite battle we fight is apathy. Apathy leaves us feeling drained and disinterested in watching the stories unfolding all around us. It expresses itself as indifference instead of scurrying from one high to the next. It sucks your energy. It actually requires a tremendous amount of focus and intentionality to find depth and meaning in the relationships and rhythms of our everyday lives. Rich life lessons surround us all the time, but routine and familiarity can camouflage them.

Apathy is like standing in our backyards and assuming we've already turned over all the stones and counted all the rocks, so it must be time to move on. In the process, we overlook the trees, flowers, and blossoming plants waiting for us to notice their beauty. It's like taking a Rock Climbing 101 class at your local gym and concluding that scaling Mt. Everest couldn't be too different. That box has been checked! Time to move on.

Apathy is not conscious neglect. Often, we just forget to pick our heads up from the daily grind and look around.

On my worst days, I feel like I'm fighting these two battles at once. I want the high of knowing what will happen during the next chapter of my life, but without the slow build-up and steady effort required to get there. I hurry past the plush, colorful settings and dynamic characters in chapter five, instead of expending the energy to study them. As a result, I miss my chance to start chapter six with richer context and fuller appreciation.

Now, of course, we can't know when we'll breathe our last breath, so we also can't know where exactly we are in our life stories. We may have years' worth of chapters remaining, we might not. But, we do know with certainty that all stories come to an end. In rare moments of clarity, I'm able to remind myself that making it to the end isn't the goal. We were created to enjoy our stories as the plot slowly reveals itself. We shouldn't have to skip ahead to the last page.

We weren't meant to write our own stories, you see. If we were, we'd know our lives' expiration dates and we'd have total control over the events that unfolded before then.

You'll discover this as you continue reading – we're not authors, we're just characters. Each one of us was created to play a specific role in a much larger, communal story about our world. This story's collective plot, which governs every part of our lives, was set in motion by God, our Creator, centuries ago. In what I'll call the "Big Story" of our world, God included two universal themes: the principle of paradox and the story framework. These two themes are the keys to discovering deeper meaning and greater purpose in the ordinary and everyday moments of our lives, including my life and your own (no backpacking trips required, by the way).

My "Oh, Shit!" Moment

- the bigger the failure, the more learning you gain -

As backward as it felt in the moment, I realized that one of my life's most meaningful lessons had just been delivered through a devastating mistake. The bigger my failure, the more colossal my loss, the more learning I gained.

———————

Once Greg and I were back stateside, my story continued in the normal workingman's world of riding a train to and from an office building each day. I worked for a consulting firm in a fancy downtown Chicago skyscraper, and I considered it my first "real job." There was a human resources team, a closet full of pens and notepads, 10 different options of coffee, and people who worked the same hours every day to take home the same paycheck every two weeks.

Before my consulting job, I helped build the sales team at a startup company that distributed branded tea. I also worked at a leadership-training nonprofit, and I'd had some other short-term gigs. This, however, was a major-league consulting firm. Our job was to provide financial valuation expertise to headlining legal cases and the law firms that handled them – Apple vs. Samsung, for example.

———

"Oh, shit."

I don't really cuss. I don't have anything against those who do, it's just not me. My friends laugh when I let a curse slip because it's something of a rarity. It wasn't a slip this time, however. I really meant it. I had screwed up big time and I felt horrible. I'd been given a tremendous amount of responsibility as a first-year consultant and I dropped the ball at the single, most critical moment of my project.

This was my "Oh, shit!" moment.

My job was to build the financial models behind the cases that vice presidents brought to the firm. Simply put - I created really, really big Excel spreadsheets that translated a bunch of raw data into one single price so that a lawyer knew how much money a certain technology or legal case was worth, and under what conditions. That doesn't sound like fun, but it was. Building financial models is like putting together a big puzzle. It was tedious work sifting through thousands of pages of deposition testimonies, corporate files, and legal documents to collect the data we needed to create the models, but once we did, I liked the intellectual challenge.

We worked as a small team. Jeff, Chris, Jon, Steve, Ashley, Ahmed and I were all pretty tight-knit. It was good to have friends in the office during those late nights. We all worked on the same cases, but after a few months on the job, a vice president, Chris, needed help with a new case from just one consultant.

The consultants who typically worked on Chris' cases were all tied up with other projects. I was known for being able to chew through large stacks of legal documents fairly quickly (I'm a fast reader) so I was given the chance to own the financial model for Chris' case. I was thrilled. It was an assignment I could build my reputation on. The case itself was intriguing, too. We were valuing the technology for a videogame system, which I found more appealing than some of the cases other consultants were stuck with (valuing parking garages or gravel piles, for example).

We had two months to produce a 100-page report and an equally large Excel model, which would be the final products for our clients. Chris would write the report and I would back up his conclusions with the financial model and corporate data.

The case progressed smoothly for the first month. The second month, I essentially lived in the office while trying to complete my work in time. I didn't really mind the long hours, however, and my roommate, Daniel, also worked late. Plus, our clients gave me permission to put dinner on their expense account if I worked more than 10 hours a day. Free food, baby! I even opted to work late some nights just to expense my dinner. I was still building my bank account balance back to five digits after my summer travels.

———

"How's that model coming along?" Jeff asked, setting a small orange basketball on my desk.

Jeff and I sat next to each other, separated by a low-profile cubicle wall. He had a picture of a fighter jet strung across one wall of his cube and a small basketball hoop stuck to the other. Whenever we needed a break, we'd take shots from different spots in the office and distract our other cube-mates.

Chris and I were about two weeks away from our deadline, so I shared with Jeff, "Pretty good. Coming along well. Chris is having me take a shot at writing some of the narrative for the report, so that's cool."

"Good stuff man, that's not supposed to happen after just a few months in your role. Nice work," Jeff encouraged me.

It was good to hear him say that. Jeff had more experience and a grueling yearlong case under his belt. It was one of the infamous war stories told around the office. He even had to leave his family's Christmas party to battle through the case that year.

"Thanks dude. Chris is making my life pretty easy – he's fun to work with. I'm diggin' it."

Jeff laughed in agreement, "I've never worked for Chris directly, but that sounds like him. Whenever he's at Lloyd's, I've never been able to buy myself or anyone else a drink. He always picks up the tab, even if he just sees you across the room and isn't sitting with you."

"Ha! Don't I know it," I grinned.

Lloyd's was the bar on the first floor of our building. I had been the beneficiary of Chris' dependable generosity many times. On half-price appetizers night, he would walk through the office to rally as many people as he could to go down to Lloyd's. There wasn't a single staff member who didn't love Chris. While there were some vice presidents who you knew would be ruthless at worst and uninteresting at best, Chris defied every stereotype. I actually enjoyed walking into his office every morning.

I continued, "You know, it's funny. To me, Chris is totally understated and humble, yet the most interesting man in the world. He speaks quietly and doesn't push any bravado across the table at you. But if you begin to ask him questions, you learn that the guy runs trails barefoot, builds drones in his garage, and races snowmobiles. I'm sure there's more I don't even know about him yet."

———

"Nate, new news. Stop by my office, okay?" Chris said as he walked by my cube.

I always appreciated that Chris was human enough to walk to my cube to talk with me. He didn't just beckon me with an email that said, "Come here. Now." I wondered what would be waiting for me behind his office door. Part of me hoped Chris had just added a new set of exotic fish to his five-foot tall tank. The realistic part of me said it couldn't be that fun.

"Hey Chris, what's up?" I asked, standing in the doorway waiting to be motioned in.

We were two days away from our project's deadline, when we'd submit the final report to our clients and the courthouse. He waved me in and brought me up to speed.

"We had some new documents sent to us overnight. The opposing counsel just released them. An amateur move – they're trying to spin our wheels with last-minute data. There could be nothing in the files, or... there could be something major in them, and they're hoping we don't find it. Either way, we have to know, and we have to know soon."

My nerves began to tingle inside me but I replied calmly, "Sure. Anything else?"

"Yeah, one more thing. Make sure someone QC's the model for us," Chris said, referring to a "quality control" process where someone outside our case double-checked my work for accuracy.

I grabbed the small, black hard drive from Chris' desk and reassured him, "Yeah, will do. Dave's helping me out with that."

I took the long way back to my desk and reassured myself I wouldn't find any bombshell documents waiting on the hard drive. Most likely, it was just a stall tactic. Besides, if there was something material lurking among the new files, we'd have the chance to argue that a last-minute document shouldn't be allowed to influence a report compiled over the course of months.

Yet, I couldn't shake the feeling that bombshell document or not, this surprise wasn't going to be a good one. I even missed what Jeff asked me as I walked by, consumed in thought.

"Hey. Hey. Hey! Nate! What was that all about?" Jeff said after managing to grab my attention.

"Oh, just a little gift from opposing counsel – more docs to go through before our report is due. You know, the one due in two days..." I filled Jeff in on the hard drive and how now, for the next 48 hours, I'd be a ball of nervous energy wondering if I had missed something important.

"Oh man, that's a bummer. Sorry about that. Can I help out?" Jeff offered.

"Eh, it's fine. It's only like another 100 files. I should be alright. Thanks though," I shrugged and plugged the new hard drive into my laptop.

———

"I think we're in decent shape – I'm going to grab a sandwich. Do you want something to eat?" I asked Chris, looking down at my watch.

My watch's gold hands told me it was 7 p.m. – five hours before our report's midnight deadline. I already knew that, though. I had been watching the clock all day to ensure I left enough time for last-minute edits. My parents gave me the watch as a gift when I first started working at the firm. It had a brown leather band and a gold-rimmed face, and I felt important and professional when I wore it.

On this particular night, however, my watch felt more like a tyrannical dictator. It was shackled to my wrist as an oppressive reminder that I wouldn't have enough time to fully review our report before submitting it. The minutes continued to melt by, counting down to our midnight deadline. I figured that if I walked out of the office to get a sandwich, I'd distract my nerves and shake the dreadful thought that I had missed some critically important detail.

Chris typed fiercely onto his keyboard. "No, I'm fine. I just need to make one final change to one of these sections based on the docs we got – you go ahead."

Chris called me shortly after I arrived back in the office with a grilled chicken panini. "Hey Nate, we're going to make a minor update to the royalty rate – can you make sure this gets changed in the model?"

I set my half-eaten chicken and tomato pita bread on his desk and I rolled the change through my spreadsheet to update the final numbers.

It was getting close to midnight. I felt a bead of hot sweat slip down my back as I read through everything one last time, scanning for typos, spelling errors, or other items that the opposing counsel might use to discredit the veracity of Chris' report. After not finding any additional tweaks, I pressed "send." Our report was officially submitted to the court and forever sealed into the legal records. It couldn't be changed, so come hell or high water, the project was done.

I eased back into my chair, believing we had completed our case. I drew a deep breath for what felt like the first time in two days and I looked at my watch again. Now, it felt more like a scoreboard, congratulating us for crossing the finish line.

"Want some?" Chris asked, wheeling his desk chair over to a case of black-labeled wine bottles in the corner of his office.

"Oh yeah! Thanks." I accepted and took a more-than-generous sip of wine well-earned. It was good wine to be sure, but it tasted even better knowing we just submitted the report for my first big case.

We began to cherish our wine but our brief stint of joyous

relief came to a screeching halt when the computer dinged with an incoming email.

"Uh, Nate…" Chris said, reading the email from our client. "The numbers in the report's final table don't match the numbers in the model. They're off. Why?"

"Oh, shit."

To this day, I'm not sure if I thought it, said it, or whispered it. I remember with certainty, however, feeling the heaviest, most crushing sinking in my stomach. I wanted that feeling to drag me down below the desk, through all 34 floors of drywall, and right into the basement where I could hide from the firestorm of anger that was sure to be unleashed on me. I had just let down the most trusting and encouraging vice president in the firm. I could own up to my own errors, but the report carried Chris' reputation. I felt like I had just jammed a knife into Chris' back.

I was red hot, trapped inside my own clothes. I wanted to run. I looked at my watch, hopelessly deliberating if I'd have enough time to make this right before Father Time declared midnight and decreed my mistake irreversible.

The silence in the room was deafening. I racked my brain for an explanation. I braced myself and came to grips with the fact that I'd watch my livelihood burn before me that night. I was marching toward the gallows. I was sure that my budding consulting career would spoil into nothingness as Chris moved

Earth itself with his pent-up rage. I had no doubt that a tsunami of vitriol had been welling up inside of Chris, and my error had just triggered his ocean of wrath.

"Okay," Chris said. "Let's go home."

I blinked.

"What?" It was all I could muster.

My initial horror transitioned into a slightly more manageable panic as I thought of solutions. I had to fix this; I was responsible. I was ready to sleep in my work clothes for the next three days, working 'round the clock to pay some type of overtime penance for the catastrophe I'd just wrought upon my boss. While fixing the report would be a quick process, I wanted Chris to unload hundreds more hours of work on me, just so I could claw my way back into good standing with him. Your reputation is everything in consulting, especially in legal settings.

"Yeah, it's time. There's nothing more for us to do tonight," Chris said before his phone rang. "Hello, this is Chris."

I couldn't hear the conversation on the other end. The phone masked the lawyer's words, which I assumed were scathing criticisms. I imagined they skipped all pleasantries and started off by yelling at Chris, "What the hell happened here?! It's in the court record now! This is permanent! We look foolish!"

Chris spoke evenly into the phone, "This is what happens

when we have documents given to us last minute, with changes in the case strategy and final edits all needed at the same time."

To my disbelief, Chris continued, "I missed it. It was my fault. I just missed this one. We'll send a redlined version tomorrow so you can resubmit it to the court."

He spoke calmly, as if he had just woken up from a nap on some office hammock. I was dumbfounded and motionless. I stared at Chris as he set the phone in its cradle. "I think I'll take a cab home tonight. It's too late for the train now. You should do the same, Nate."

I couldn't believe it. Chris had accepted the blame for my mistake, flat out. No yelling, no crippling amount of extra work, no saving himself by casting the first-year consultant to the wolves. Somehow, he was genuinely concerned that I made it home safely.

"Uh, okay. But what can I do to help out tonight?" I asked once more. I knew I wouldn't be able to fall asleep without doing something to dig myself out of my hole. I didn't want grace to come that easily, you see.

"Go home Nate. There's nothing more for us to do tonight. Sleep," Chris ordered.

———

Do you remember how we said in the preface that stories keep things simple? That stories and the principle of paradox help us discover greater meaning in our everyday lives? This is never more visible than against the backdrop of our greatest failures, which often leave us confused and frustrated.

There has never been a perfect person in the history of stories. Well, at least in the history of interesting stories. Characters inevitably screw up as the plot unfolds, and a story's core conflict is always rooted in the main character's shortcomings. This is crucial because we all crave to see conflict resolved. Imperfect characters keep us engaged, sitting in a movie theater or reading a book for hours.

If not outright failure, at the very minimum, we prefer the characters we watch to have some type of personality flaw or past regret plaguing them. We relate to wounded characters. We root for them to pull through in the end because it mirrors our own experiences – we're not perfect people either. I mean, can you imagine reading a book about someone who does everything right, and faces no opposition whatsoever? Of course not. We'd either tear the book in two before finishing it, or we'd finish it and feel like losers by comparison.

The same concept applies to our daily lives. While we shy away from conflict and we fear failure, these experiences serve as open doors to grace, growth, and new lessons learned. We mature as we deal with the fallout from our mistakes. We become more interesting characters. If we can accept – and in fact, demand – flawed characters as critical to the stories we watch and read, we must learn to do the same in our own lives instead of viewing failure as *a fait accompli*. This perspective is the path to finding greater meaning in our most frustrating letdowns and confusing defeats.

———

I sat in a cab watching Jimmy Kimmel Live on the back of the passenger seat. It was helpful to focus on something other than spreadsheets, lawyers, and office buildings. I turned to watch the city lights stream by as the cabbie turned down Orleans, crossing the Chicago River. The city was still wide awake at 1:00 a.m. I wondered if the shadowy outlines in office windows were people huddled over Word documents, meticulously checking their work into the early hours of the morning to ensure they were error-free for tomorrow's presentations.

"How do you screw up as a cab driver?" I thought to myself, legitimately considering a career change. I debated if I'd be able to sit in a car for 10 hours a day and decided against it. Crashing into other cars for half the salary didn't feel like a good trade.

The cabbie pulled up to my apartment and I tipped him double. He'd driven me home accident-free and it's not every day, after all, that you get your job done without screwing it up.

I slid out from the back seat and walked into my apartment before dropping my keys into a wooden bowl. A loud, clanging noise echoed from our 15-foot tall ceilings. I wanted to wake up my roommate, Daniel, just so that he could ask me about my day. Then I'd have someone to commiserate with. No sound came from his room, however. I didn't have a choice. Maybe it was best to go to bed pretending it was a normal day.

I crumpled into my sheets and rolled onto my back with a groan. As my eyes adjusted to the dark, I tried to grasp what exactly I should have been learning from my mistake. While I had screwed up before – hurt people I loved, failed exams, and other run-of-the-mill missteps – I had never fallen flat in such a way that I directly torpedoed someone else's reputation, with the entire blame landing squarely on me. I racked my brain for some type of lesson to help me move forward and avoid repeating one of my most public failures.

Sleep evaded me as I stared at the ceiling's plastered ridges and grooves. I ruminated over Chris so calmly instructing me, "Go home Nate. There's nothing more for us to do tonight." Those words haunted me. They didn't offer any opportunity to atone for what I'd done. I botched our report in the grandest of fashions, yet Chris had no less respect for me. He treated me no differently. I couldn't make heads or tails of it.

As backward as it felt in the moment, I discovered that one of my life's most meaningful lessons had just been delivered in the form of a devastating mistake. The bigger my failure, the more colossal my mistake, the more learning I gained.

What's more, Chris embodied a perfect picture of grace. He had entrusted me with our report, granting me full autonomy and responsibility. Still, I fell short. I missed the mark. There was no way I'd be able to repay him, and I knew that even if I could, he wouldn't have allowed it. Chris readily accepted the blame for my error as soon as he discovered it. He showed me that the harder we fall, the more grace we receive.

In the same way, the collective story of our world, the "Big Story," says that our author (God) didn't create flawless characters (us) who produce error-free reports. Instead, He knew imperfect characters who can decide to love Him or walk away from Him, choosing conflict and a broken relationship, make for a better story. Knowing full well we'd fail, our Creator not only proceeded to write us into existence, He made grace central to our story's resolving event – death on a wooden cross we built for his son over 2,000 years ago.

In my finest moments, that sentence, "Go home, Nate. There's nothing more to do tonight," rings out when I'm affected by a friend, colleague, or family member's mistake. Chris helped me see that if I've been given a second chance, how can I demand perfection from someone else? I try to ask myself in moments of mindfulness and my own missteps: what's the lesson hiding behind this failure?

The Story of a Hero (You)

October 2014

- it's the ordinary people who become our biggest heroes -

Our heroes always start out as regular guys. If you saw someone
who was born into paranormal circumstances or with some
supernatural ability, you'd expect them to show up... but
our real heroes start as everyday people.

I felt antsy after another eight months at the consulting firm. I was working on a new case with a larger team and I was performing really well, but I wanted something different. My work had become too structured. I was confined to the narrow lanes of financial models and lawyers and I longed to explore other areas of business. So, I began making arrangements to launch my own startup company.

The startup process gave me newfound energy. I was invigorated by the unknowns inherent to founding a company. I woke up excited each day despite staying out until midnight at different events around Chicago's startup scene. It became easier to find purpose in my daily routines.

I also took up training for an Ironman triathlon after my last case with Chris. After being enclosed in the four walls of our office every day, I needed an outlet. My roommate, Daniel, said he was up for the adventure, too. He's ultra-competitive, so there was no way he'd have let me tackle the challenge alone. This is a guy who's never lost a game of backyard football in his career, not only because he's the fastest one on the field, but because he can't stand to let someone else beat him.

Daniel and I rode our bike to the gym, lifted weights, and swam before riding to our respective consulting firms each morning. My attire became more and more casual that spring (I went from the office's typical business slacks to Gap khakis) and I billed less time to clients. When I wasn't training, I spent time at long lunches with potential investors, business partners, and other entrepreneurs to develop my idea for a startup.

In late June, I met an entrepreneur named Brian for lunch. Earlier that week, a mutual friend had said to me, "You know, I think Brian's a guy you could work with; I'll introduce you two." Brian wore blue wood glasses and had an enchanting charisma about him. There was a magnetism in the way he spoke and the words he chose. When I pitched him the company I wanted to build, he quickly sold me on his idea instead. He was creating a platform that would help small nonprofits without full-time fundraising staff raise enough money to expand their programs and impact.

Two weeks later, I decided I was in. I'd leave my consulting firm to help Brian build the dream. I met him for lunch once more to talk about details, ownership, and what papers I needed to put my John Hancock on. Two weeks after that (my one-year anniversary at the firm no less), I left my consulting job to start working on our new venture.

Brian and I hit it off immediately. Our complimentary personalities made us perfect co-founders. Brian generally ignores schedules and deadlines while I obsess over hitting goals and staying on target. He sees the vision; I see the process. We both see the world through rose-colored lenses, and we became fast friends outside the office. I also continued training for October's Ironman race as I opened this entirely new chapter of my life. I packed my days full of life as an entrepreneur-triathlete.

I liked the pace of my life. I was single and uninterested in dating. I was content to work, train, eat Thai food, and repeat. At a certain point, my neighborhood Thai restaurant even knew my phone number. I'd call to place a takeout order as soon as I'd leave our office in the Chicago Loop. I'd ask Pauly, the hostess, how her night was going, and I'd let her know that I'd be by the restaurant in 15 minutes. If Daniel was working late, I'd order for two. I actually liked my routine for the first time in my life. I was working toward two big goals, building a company and racing triathlons, and that was energizing.

———

I opened my eyes and grabbed my phone to look at the time – 4:30 a.m. I realized what day it was and I felt awake enough to get out of bed. It was October 5th. Race day. I climbed down from the top bunk and peeked into the bottom to see what state of being Daniel was in. It was early, so he was still asleep. The day couldn't have come quickly enough for me. I couldn't stay in bed.

We were in a small, European-style Airbnb in Calella, Spain. It was tucked into the third floor of a building only accessible on foot. The roads in Calella are too narrow to drive cars. Aside from three main strips that cars can access, Calella is a quaint pedestrian-only coastal town with unique food and family-run corner stores. On this particular weekend, blue Ironman flags were hung in every window.

I walked into the kitchen and grabbed a container of baby formula from the shelf. I spooned out two scoops of the formula into some warm water, mixed it together, and tasted the first part of my pre-race breakfast. It didn't taste very good. I needed the extra calories, however, and the formula wouldn't give my stomach any digestive issues (a triathlete's worst enemy).

I stepped onto our balcony with my milk. The balcony wasn't spacious, four square feet at most, but it was enough to get outside and feel the weather. It was raining so hard I could hear a loud slap as each drop hit the cobblestone streets below me. Later that morning, Daniel and I would start our 140.6-mile journey up and down Barcelona's coastal highways and Calella's narrow beachfront paths. The rain brought a palpable humidity despite the strong morning breeze. I wondered if it would let up before the race started.

"Should have expected rain," I mumbled, stepping back inside.

"Morning, Pops," I said as my dad emerged from his bedroom.

He reached high up into the air to stretch away the nighttime stiffness, grinning as he did so. He's always had this distinctive smile in the morning. It's like the day is full of secrets to him, treasures he can't wait to unearth. I imagined his stretch was just him practicing for the finish line. I knew he'd be there waiting for me, smiling with his fists raised high in the air as I ran down the finisher's chute. He'd certainly flown a long way for one race but he'd always been there for me growing up. It felt right to have him with me on race day.

"Well, it's raining," I informed him.

"Oh man, I forgot my rain suit," he groaned, walking into the kitchen. "What a drag."

I laughed, knowing what he meant. He wasn't disappointed it was raining. He was just sad to miss the perfect chance to break out his bright green rain gear. To put this in perspective, my dad loves gear. Gear of all kinds. He says there's no such thing as bad circumstances. Just unprepared people without the right tools.

A few years earlier, my dad flew to Knoxville, Tennessee, to watch my first triathlon. I was racing 70 miles with a fever in pouring, 50-degree rain on a flooded racecourse. He stood outside for the whole race, smiling in that luminous green rain suit and running the last quarter mile with me. I had wanted to tell my dad how grateful I was that he was there – just like he always was – but I couldn't talk very well. My voice was barely audible after racing in the rain with a 101-degree fever for almost six hours. Even if my voice was working properly, I'm not sure I could have properly articulated how I felt.

I was having the same challenge that morning in Calella. I wanted him to know how grateful I was to be standing with him in that little Spanish kitchen. I felt peaceful, more confident because he was there with me. It wouldn't have felt like race day without him.

Before I could think of the right thing to say, Daniel declared he was awake, "Well, I'm going to drown before I make it out of the water, so we might as well just get this thing started!"

The pitch of his trademark laugh rose above the roar of the rainstorm outside. I dismissed his doom and gloom, knowing full well he'd finish the race in great shape. Daniel's nerves always spiral into a verbal panic of the most impossible, defeating scenarios, and how they'll surely get the best of him. I was glad he shares his thoughts out loud, though; it gave me a chance to shoot down the negativity.

"Want some?" I asked, handing him the baby formula.

"Nope," he said, grabbing my glass. "But I'll drink it anyway."

———

"Hey Pops, can you toss me that bar?" I pointed to the coconut chocolate granola bar in the pocket of his backpack.

I looked out at the ocean and watched the stormy waves rise and fall as the sun crept over the horizon. The race's start time had been delayed by over an hour at this point. The lightning was beginning to dissipate too. I was hopeful we'd be able start our race soon.

"I've already peed in my wetsuit twice. I'll have nothing left in the tank by the time we start this thing!" Daniel exclaimed, pointing to the wet sand around him.

I laughed because it was true. We'd been sitting in our wetsuits for too long. I was trying to munch on food and drink water as we waited for the weather to pass. I wasn't sure what felt more tumultuous – the waves stirred up by the storm, or a few hundred high-strung triathletes impatiently waiting to tear into the course.

"The radar shows everything clearing in 20 minutes," my dad

said, handing me his backpack. "You guys should be good to go soon. I'll get your shoes and jackets home after you start. Need me to do anything else?"

"Nope, I think we're set. Thanks for hanging out, Pops."

We heard a megaphone blare from a few yards down the beach, "Attention athletes. Be advised. Due to weather delays, we're cutting the course time limits by two hours. Your swim course cutoff will remain the same, but both the bike and run courses will pull athletes off one hour earlier, with 15 total hours allowed. Thank you!"

"Awesome. A good mental pre-race boost," Daniel laughed.

I kept my mind occupied and touched the tattoo, "2 Corinthians 4:16-18" running down my inner forearm. "So we do not lose heart... for this light, momentary affliction is preparing for ourselves an eternal weight of glory beyond all comparison...'"

———

I was beginning to drone. Droning is when your mind fades in and out, but your body keeps moving forward. You're no longer actively thinking when you drone. You can even forget what's happened in the last few moments, despite the fact you're still technically awake and pressing onward. I was on mile 18 of the marathon at this point. No man's land. Mile 18 of the run course is mile 132 of the overall Ironman course, so I was far enough along that I couldn't give up, but I was far enough away from the finish that sweet relief felt unattainable.

I turned away from Calella's spectator circle to head down the darkening, empty beach trail for my final eight miles. I was feeling fine physically (relatively speaking). I had raced smart and set a good pace, fueling up along the way. I could tell I wasn't getting enough sugars to my brain, however. My thoughts came and went as my body craved glucose but I just couldn't stomach another packet of fruity energy gel. I had probably ingested 20 of them in the last 10 hours.

"Way to go, sonny-boy!" I heard my Dad yell, looking out from behind his camera.

I heard him before I saw him. He was crouched down with his camera, taking one final shot before the last rays of sunlight left us. He had been sitting there for the last hour, waiting for me to run by, smiling the whole time. I decided then that I didn't have to suffer down another sport gel. My dad gave me a greater mental boost than any squeezable packet of sugar could.

———

"Sorry about your shoes, guys. I thought I could dry them out but it didn't work out so well," my dad handed me a melted Nike running shoe.

I had to laugh. After leaving the beach at the start of the race, he took our rain-soaked clothes and shoes back to our Airbnb and stuck them in the dryer before walking to the finish line. He figured that after hours of standing and racing in the rain, we'd appreciate some dry, warm clothes. The problem, however, was that the dryer had heated up our shoes past their melting point and it totally fried the soles. They melted and then re-hardened into a deformed, unusable shape.

I tried to force one of my shoes back into its original form but it proved to be a fool's errand. It snapped back into an awkwardly curved shape. "I'll pay for a new pair," my dad offered quickly. I could tell he thought he'd just ruined our post-race celebration.

I reassured him, "Thanks, but no need. You flew here by yourself to stand outside for 12 hours. In the rain, no less. That means more to me than shoes ever will."

He smiled again, relenting, "Alright, but at least let me buy you dinner tomorrow."

"That's a deal."

The fact that my dad had traveled all the way to Spain just to cheer me on amazed me. Yes, he was my dad, but still. He could have used the time to do something for himself. He depleted his vacation time and allowed work and his other responsibilities to stack up back home. He even insisted on paying his fair share of our meals and Airbnb's. After countless years of being there for me, he could have let me treat him for once. Heck, he could have just woken up early to send me a good luck text message from the comfort of his own bed in the U.S. Instead, he was right there by my side.

He was my hero.

————

We packed up our race gear and drove down the coast to Barcelona after a long night of randomly waking up to quench our bodies' cravings for more food. We planned to hang around the city for a few days before shipping our gear back to the U.S. and flying to Brussels to tour more of Europe. As our shuttle driver navigated down the coastal highway, I opened the book I had started reading on the flight over. It was called *Orthodoxy* by GK Chesterton. Although it was dense, I liked Chesterton's writing. He's one of those writers who makes you re-read every page to make sure you've caught everything.

Orthodoxy is, in a way, a book about Chesterton's own story. He uses his autobiography to outline a rational case for belief in a God, an Author of life, by recounting memories and examples from his own life. Each chapter details a season of his life that ultimately swayed him to move from an atheistic, self-sufficient worldview to faith in a divine Creator. In one section, Chesterton details the role that fairy tales and imagination played in his conversion, and I came to a section in which he muses about the concept of heroes:

> The old fairy tales make the hero a normal human boy; it is his

adventures that are startling; they startle him because he is normal. You can make a story out of a hero among dragons; but not out of a dragon among dragons.[i]

As I looked up from my book and watched my dad sitting in the front seat, Chesterton's proposition made sense to me. True heroes do always start out as normal, regular guys. If you saw someone who was born into paranormal circumstances or with some supernatural ability, you'd expect them to show up in the ways they had been born to. Saving lives, helping cats trapped on rooftops during a flood - that kind of stuff. Our real heroes start out as everyday people. They're ordinary humans who face life alongside us with unfailing courage, consistency, and smiles.

As we drove on, I thought about how my dad always came through for me. When I first signed up for the race, I figured there was a slim chance he would fly to Barcelona. I assumed it would be the first time he'd be forced to support me from afar. Yet, there he was. Sitting in our shuttle, smiling and watching the coastline roll by.

My dad and mom, together, have helped me reach every victory in my life. They're the quiet heroes behind every achievement to my name. By most standards, people will say that co-founding a company and competing in Ironman-distance triathlons are impressive accomplishments. While I'd never wave that flag, it would be easy to let people believe I've attained these things under my grit and determination alone.

That wouldn't be accurate, however. The truth is that my heroes empowered me to do those things.

Growing up, I was given the chance to travel, play sports, try new things, and graduate with a college degree debt-free. The opportunities my childhood afforded me – all enabled by my parents – forged a fearlessness in me. Through each experience, my parents reinforced that I could be whatever I set out to be. Whether that was an athlete (as they took pictures at my soccer games and made me feel like the most important player) or an entrepreneur (they paid me $5 to cook dinner and let me draw menus while pretending our kitchen was a restaurant), they always told me, "Go for it, Nate."

To this day, I approach life with an undying optimism and firm belief that everything will work out just fine because my parents took on so many of the typical childhood worries for me. When I quit my consulting job, co-founded a company debt-free, and bought a bike to race an Ironman despite dealing with chronic asthma and anemia, I felt more grateful than ever.

My heroes came through once again.

―――

Everyone is looking for a hero. Everybody wants some type of life-giving and affirming presence in their story at the very least. That's just how our Author designed us.

When we come to understand that we're all characters who

play a small role in the Big Story of our world, we see why we're drawn into the popular Hollywood-hero storyline. We turn out in droves to watch someone really impressive and good-looking swoop down to save the day because it's part of who we are.

A book in the Bible explains this. Genesis documents the history of our creation, and it gives us a reference point to grasp just how far we've strayed from God's original design. Genesis tell us that we like to control the storyline, ignoring our Author's instructions, and when we try to direct the narrative on our own we screw up and find ourselves in need of saving. Our need for a savior dates all the way back to Adam and Eve.

We all need different heroes because we all have different life perspectives. From your vantage point, you feel what you need and want in life. So, your hero will be someone who reflects that. My heroes come in different forms, however, because I have a different life story. The common denominator between us is that our true heroes always begin as ordinary people.

While celebrities and world leaders can certainly be considered heroes in their own right, greater meaning, connection, and influence always comes from the everyday heroes who are closest to us – mentors, parents, coaches, etc. We may admire the people we watch on TV and never meet, but rarely will they shape our lives in a truly profound way.

Now, if we can accept this idea of a creation story – that we're all part of God's Big Story and our world of intellect, emotion, and morality wasn't formed by a random, cosmic accident – we can define our heroes as those who shape our character in the Big Story for good.

C.S. Lewis' *The Weight of Glory* confirms this, and it lays out an interesting consideration. Lewis says:

> [E]very time you make a choice you are turning the central part of you, the part of you that chooses, into something a little different than it was before. And taking your life as a whole, with all your innumerable choices, all your life long you are slowly turning this central thing into a heavenly creature or a hellish creature... Each of us at each moment is progressing to the one state or the other.[ii]

Lewis is pointing out that we're not static beings. People are much more complex than that. Characters all develop as the plotline progresses and we, as characters in the Big Story, also change in one direction or another. Over the course of many years, the people we interact with either push us in the direction of joy and harmony with our story's Creator, or they push us towards hate and a state of war with our Creator.

Therefore, if we begin to see our heroes as the people who influence our stories in a heavenly way, we have a new standard for how we define who is (and is not) a hero. We'll also have a standard to define who the ultimate Hero (capital "H") of our story is – the one who can restore us to a heavenly state, completely and eternally, at the end of our lives.

Besides, if only the one-time, exceptional feats are our metrics for identifying who our heroes are, how will we ever feel we've arrived? Daily routines, predictable responsibilities, dishes, bills, and to-do lists don't preclude us from extraordinary action. We just need to reframe what we define as the essentials for heroism.

Here's the driving point behind all this. Although it feels backward, being the ordinary 'you' is actually the prerequisite for becoming someone's hero. It's also important to recognize how your heroes have shaped your life for the better.

So, would you consider yourself a hero?

I don't consider myself a hero, and if I were to hazard a guess, I'd say you most likely feel, "Of course not, I'm just (insert first name here)." But if a hero doesn't need a cape, and we can find heroes among ordinary people who step up to positively influence our lives, there's nothing stopping you from becoming someone's hero, right?

Tacos & Tree Talk

March 2015

- paradox is the norm, not the exception in life -

As I watched him, I knew those things didn't matter. The storm stirring inside me, juxtaposed against Michael's calm, said so.

———————

After arriving stateside from our post-race travels, Daniel and I received word from Team USA's Long Course Triathlon director. We had qualified to race with our age-group team during the 2015 World Championships in Motala, Sweden. We didn't need to consider the opportunity; we signed on immediately.

Before diving back into training, we took three months out of the pool and let our bikes sit idle. It was a nice break, but somehow, my work absorbed all the hours I would have spent training. Our company was growing and for all seven days every week, if I didn't have something planned, I'd gravitate to my laptop and return to emails and projects.

I needed a mid-week reprieve from my intense work and training schedule. Fortunately, one day after church, a guy named Michael asked if I'd be interested in meeting to talk about the Bible and building businesses. It seemed like an interesting combination of topics so I said I was in. Michael connected me with a group of entrepreneurs from different places around the city and we all started meeting for breakfast on Wednesdays.

———

It was early. The city streets were still empty. I locked up my bike in front of the Union League Club, tucked my helmet into my backpack, and unfolded my jeans. I zipped up my orange pullover and walked past the Club's front revolving doors. I stepped into the alleyway where the service entrance was located and cracked the door. I studied the front entrance and spotted the doorman. As he turned and diverted his gaze, I swept into the Great Room and bee-lined to the elevator. I held the 'Close' button down before anyone could stop me.

The Union League Club wasn't really my scene. The dress code was too strict. If the doorman stopped me wearing jeans and a hoody, he'd send me right to the "lost and found." It was really just a pile of clothes from the 1980's that Club members had left in the locker room (intentionally, I imagine). Then, I'd be forced to pull on a pair of old slacks. That happened to me once. I was caught wearing jeans and the pair of pants I was given to wear were ten years out of style and five sizes too large.

Once out of the elevator, I made my way down a short hallway filled with expensive paintings. I settled into a lavish, leather-backed chair surrounded by mahogany shelving and a massive stone fireplace. It was the kind of room that reminded me of political shows, or oil barons. It was where powerful senators, state leaders, and "old money" all sit to joke about the normal, inconsequential people of our world in a plume of cigar smoke.

As Nate – another Nate – poured me a cup of coffee, I shook Tim's hand. I said hey to Michael, Matt, Hank, and we waited for Mike to show up. We met in the same room every week. Each of us needed those mornings. Being entrepreneurs, we all rode emotional roller coasters while developing our respective projects or products that were always more demanding than rewarding. Michael and I were both focused on nonprofits and technology while the others were in finance, real estate, media, and restaurants.

We had our own ritual. While we'd wait for Mike to walk in 20 minutes late, Michael would serve as our group's shaman and kick off the conversation with a certain discussion topic. As we talked, the other Nate would ask some type of existential, thought-stirring question like, "How can there be evil in the world if God is good?" We'd all think on that for a few moments. You couldn't tame Nate's curiosity. I appreciated his questions but Tim, Hank, and I didn't always know how to respond. Matt would then break the silence with some sarcastic comment.

Michael would reel the conversation in and we'd listen intently again. Then, Mike would walk into the room and crack a joke. We'd laugh, welcome him, and move on to the next topic.

This morning was different, however. Michael started off by sharing he'd be moving back home to his parents' house in the suburbs. He was out of cash and waiting for more funding to fuel his startup. He said he planned to use his in-between time to work at McDonald's and share God's love with his new co-workers. He was looking forward to an easier pace of life with more time to meditate. That sounded pretty radical to us, but if anybody would choose that path and thrive, it was Michael.

Before leaving the Club that morning, I promised myself I'd visit Michael in the suburbs. I enjoyed talking with him. More so, I enjoyed listening as he responded to my questions with profound, God-given wisdom. I didn't want that to change just because he wasn't living in the city anymore.

———

Michael had been living in the suburbs for a few months when March rolled around. I decided to check in and see if he was interested in meeting up for tacos, which he was. We met at the tail-end of a particularly demanding stretch of life for me. I had been working for nearly three months without a full day off as Brian and I drove the company forward by brute force, hacking together everything from new marketing initiatives to product developments. We even started renting Airbnb's in remote forest locations just to work outside the city on weekends.

I was keeping up my training schedule for the big race in Sweden, too. While I loved my breakneck pace, I also knew I needed to find some rest. Dinner with Michael seemed to be just what I needed. We ordered tacos and without much delay, I asked Michael what he was learning about rest and restoration through his time in the suburbs. I knew he wanted to find more peace outside the city, and without the hustle of managing his company's product launches and coding sprints.

Michael started talking about trees. He'd sit on his parents' patio in the mornings to listen to the sound of the wind rustling the leaves and to watch the bright red cardinals flying across the yard. It was soothing to him. Then he started to talk about something much more profound.

"I'm also learning about resurrection, or at least I'm supposed to be learning about resurrection," Michael said, dragging a handful of tortilla chips through salsa.

"Like, dead things coming to life? That kind of resurrection?"

"Right, and how the Bible's story of resurrection plays out in our lives." Michael paused to swallow his chips before continuing, "It's a pretty relevant topic because our company has essentially died. We're out of cash. We hibernated our website, and now we're waiting for a new round of investment

– a resurrection – to begin operating again."

As Michael continued to talk about resurrection, he used the word "paradox" to describe how the foundational truths governing our lives show up in ways that feel very backward to us. He said our Creator, in His infinite knowledge, wrote a story with a script we never could have guessed.

"Give me an example of that, truth showing up backward," I challenged more curiously than defensively. I set my pork taco down to focus on what Michael was saying.

"Well, it's all throughout Jesus' teachings and what we have recorded in scripture. Think about how Jesus said the poor will inherit the world, or how the first will be last and the last will be first," Michael explained.

"More practically, think about how death gives way to life in trees."

I laughed, "Trees? In what way?"

"Trees are actually dying as they lose their leaves. The tree has to conserve its energy for winter, so it kills its leaves by breaking down the chlorophyll in them. Then it sheds them to the ground. In the process of dying, the leaves change colors and we get something new and even more magnificent – a tree full of yellow, red, orange, even a whole season called 'fall.' Then, life 'springs' forth as the tree survives winter. There's something beautifully backward about that. Death as the passage to life."

Our tacos went down easy, but it would take me a while to fully digest Michael's words.

———

Only the Author knows what will unfold in any given chapter of a story. In the same way, because I'm limited to my role as "Nate" in the Big Story of our world, my life's most confusing moments only end up making sense over the long-term. After I've continued to live life forward, I can look backward and understand more in hindsight. I can re-read the script. Greater context affords clarity, and it helps me uncover the meaning underpinning frustrating experiences.

We're characters, not authors, so we won't always understand the "why" behind our experiences as we live them. But, if we realize that paradox is actually the norm and not the exception in the Big Story of our world, we'll learn to study our confusing and ordinary moments more closely. We'll begin to ask, "Why?" instead of, "Why me?"

Before eating tacos with Michael, I had never used the word paradox in a sentence, let alone considered how it may influence my life. Yet, the principle still applied. Here's a quick example of what I mean.

Years before our dinner, I was turned down for an elite consulting job. I had prepared hours upon hours for the interview process and I had made it past 500 candidates to the final three. I even ranked highest on the business problems we were given to solve during the last of a four-part hiring process.

Then, somehow, they gave the job to the guy who bombed his last interviews. I remember hanging up the phone feeling shocked and confused. More accurately, I was pissed. But, years later, I came to appreciate that plot twist. That job would have taken me out of Chicago and I never would have found my call as an entrepreneur. What's more, I'd never have met my wife.

Because I was infuriated in the moment, I didn't look to the bigger storyline unfolding; I saw no purpose behind the rejection. Had I known that life often unfolds a little differently than we first expect, I'd have understood that rejection was actually a gift. That denial was a blessing. Now, that doesn't make much sense on the surface, but over time, I found a more significant life with my wife and as an entrepreneur.

———

I put my taco back in my mouth and considered my options. If I agreed with Michael, what he was telling me would require a shift in my thinking. I didn't find that very desirable. I wanted to keep my own storyline as the center of the world, with my own pursuits and ambitions as the focal point. I wanted to narrate and decide how my story developed, cherry-picking the elements of religion and Christianity that I found convenient.

But Michael told me that Jesus' death and resurrection – the

Gospel story – is actually the main story of our world. He said its truths are reflected in our daily lives. He said that if I looked for it, I'd see the Gospel story showing up in my life in ways I didn't expect (as paradox).

Candidly, I thought Michael was nuts. He sounded pretty far out there. But, I considered the possibilities as he continued talking. I did believe that Jesus was a real, living person who walked this Earth. I also believed the historical evidence points to his death and subsequent resurrection. But did that translate to bigger things for my life? No. Not really. I wanted to live life as I wanted to now and worry about everything else when I died.

Ravi Zacharias is a Christian apologist who says there are four major questions in everyone's life – origin, meaning, morality, and destiny. Everyone's worldview – Atheist, Buddhist, Muslim, Agnostic, Jew – posits an answer to these four questions. Where did we come from? Why are we here? Am I a good person? Where am I going?

According to Ravi's framework, I had been justifying my life by applying my worldview to two of these four questions – origin and destiny. I figured that if my faith told me how I got here (creation vs. evolution) and where I was going after (eternal life vs. annihilation), what does faith really have to do with how I live here on Earth? In other words, I had no choice but to accept the start and end dates of my life but I wanted to define the "dash" in-between.

It was my mental shortcut. It let me live in bliss. I could derive my own "meaning" and "morality," as Mr. Zacharias would say, without some divine author directing me. I wanted to direct why I was living and to what end while defining if I was doing a good job of that. Truth doesn't bend to our preferences, however. It permeates all corners of our lives whether we like it or not.

I loaded another tortilla chip with guacamole and kept thinking. As I did, Michael's continued tree-talk broke through my neat dividing lines. He continued to talk about the greatest paradox of all time; full and eternal life was offered to everyone when Jesus died on a cross. Death was the passageway to a meaningful, moral life here on Earth.

I needed to change the topic. I didn't enjoy feeling that my lifestyle was on trial. Looking back, I realize that Michael wasn't calling me out in the slightest, I simply felt convicted. So, I lobbed him a few easy questions about working at McDonald's, living at home, and some lighter topics.

As I faded between my thoughts and Michael's words, I noticed something different about him. You know how there are those scenes in movies where someone is talking, and you see their mouth moving, but you don't hear the words? Only the thoughts in the protagonist's head?

This was like that. "Why does he look so calm?" I asked myself. There was a peace about him I hadn't seen before. He looked rested, he spoke vibrantly, and he had a certain tranquility about him. Maybe he only looked extra peaceful in contrast to my own worn-down spirit that day. I couldn't help feeling, however, that between the two of us, Michael was the one who was truly living.

All of our society's values and ideals screamed, "that can't be!" How was it that in a time when Michael was broke, working at McDonald's, and living with his parents, he seemed less anxious than I was? I was the one leading a growing company with plenty of access to cash and investors; I drove a car and he walked; I picked up our dinner tab; I was going to sleep in a nice downtown loft while he was headed to sleep in his childhood bedroom.

By all measures, I was the one who should have felt inner peace. At the same time, as I watched him, I knew those things didn't matter. The storm stirring inside me, juxtaposed against Michael's calm, said so.

At the end of the evening, I asked Michael if I could give him a lift home. He said he preferred to walk. It was a nice night and walking would give him some time alone. So we said goodbye and I started up my car.

As I drove onto the highway's entrance ramp to head back into Chicago, my eye caught something that seemed out of place. As I was winding around the ramp's curve, there was a wolf limping across the ramp. He looked back at me with piercing, blue eyes.

His coat was magnificent – a rich grey and white waving in the wind like a wheat field on the Kansas plains. There was something striking about him. He gave me the kind of feeling that makes you hold your breath before letting it out in the form of "woah." He walked with a limp, raising his front right paw that glimmered with a bright red streak across his white fur.

I took my foot off the accelerator to make sure I was actually seeing what I thought I was seeing. As I slowed, he vanished down the bank of the ramp and I lost him.

"Uh, what?" I said out loud. Maybe I hadn't seen anything?

No, I definitely saw a wolf. He was as real as the tacos I had just polished off.

Clearly, a wolf of that caliber was out of place on a city expressway. Not only was he out of place, he was hurt. A thought came to me: the wolf was a symbol, representing a man who had been lost in the world and he was trying to find his way back home. In his search, he began pursuing things that didn't matter, pushing him further away from home until he was injured in the process.

It was a strange moment, but to be honest, writing about it is much stranger. Putting this into written word reinforces its reality. This kind of stuff doesn't usually happen to me.

I asked myself again, "Was that an actual sign, or is this just in my head?"

Seconds later, I passed a massive green sign that stretched over the highway and read "Wolf Road." Wouldn't you know it? It wasn't just undercooked flank steak in my tacos. I was being asked to put more time and thought into the importance of my conversation with Michael instead of dismissing it. I suppressed my rising instinct to chalk everything up to coincidence and I thought about why I worked so hard, and what I was giving up in the process. I played out the trajectory of my life. I thought about who I'd become if I continued in the same way for a few more years.

I considered how I'd just worked 90 days straight. I realized that in the process of gaining a career, a company, and to be honest, an identity I really liked as an "entrepreneur," I was also giving up time with my family and friends.

Selfishly, I had been focusing on my own ambitions and I had forgotten about the relationships and characters who had played an influential role in my life. Close to a month had passed since I had called my mom just to say hello. I had no idea what was happening in my brother's or sisters' lives. I hadn't stopped by the family house to catch up with my dad.

Those were things I could have done while keeping a busy schedule, but I was too caught up living another story. I wasn't malicious; I was just consumed. I hadn't looked me around until Michael clued me into the big picture. You see, neglect is what happens when characters mistake themselves for authors – they wrap themselves up too heavily in the sub-plot. We start to believe we're the whole story, or that the world hinges on the story we're living.

Well, maybe not you. I do that too often.

I decided to text my dad, "Hey Pops, want to get dinner next week?" Fast forward one week, we did get dinner. And do you know what? It's one of the most memorable meals I've ever shared with someone. I can still recall what we talked about, at which table we sat, and what we ordered. For a short while, I felt a sense of calm return. I wasn't trying to do more or go faster. I found meaning in simply sitting and sharing life with my dad. I knew he enjoyed being with me, too.

It's nice to know you mean something to the people you love just because of who you are, not what you've accomplished.

If you believe there's a Big Story that brings meaning to your life, but you've been a little too wrapped up in your own story lately, who could you ask out for tacos? If you don't believe there's a Big Story to our world, where do you look for meaning? What matters most in your life?

Choppin' Trees

April 2015

- we find true rest while we're still at work -

"We value each other by how much we're needed. How busy, how tired we are. In fact, we fear what rest will cost us – our identity."

– Jason Helveston

———————

Trees seemed to be a topic of conversation that kept springing up. I was talking about trees once more just a few weeks later. Our Wednesday morning breakfast club disbanded soon after Michael moved to the suburbs, and I went back to craving deeper discussions about life during the workweek. You can only think about work for so many hours before you need to give your mind a break. I wasn't dating anyone, so I didn't have much outlet for other conversations.

I eventually asked two good friends, Mo and Sam, to start meeting me after work. We'd eat dinner and talk about stories in the Bible. Although they lived pretty far north, we met in the city most weeks. I was thankful for that. I needed those nights.

———

"Do you ever feel like you're just trying to chop down trees in life?" Sam asked us.

I was sitting across from Sam in a small café. Like most weeks we met, Sam had taken an hour-long, one-way train ride into the city. His roundtrip travel lasted longer than our conversation that night. I wondered if he came just to ask that question.

I tuned out the guy arguing with the barista and picked up what Sam was hinting, "Yeah, I guess so. I mean, it's pretty tiring to chop down trees, right?"

I laughed to myself. Chopping down an actual tree couldn't be very hard for Sam. He eats six eggs and two avocados with bacon for breakfast and has biceps bigger than my thighs. I knew what he meant, though. He was referring to the "proverbial tree." It was a metaphor for the daily grind and endless to-do list that life throws at us, and how we have to chip away at them one by one.

Mo turned in his chair to face us. "What kind of trees are we talking about here? You look tired Sam, what's up?"

Sam doesn't use more words than he needs. He doesn't freely offer his opinion if you don't ask, so Mo pressed the issued.

Sam gave in and replied, "Yeah Mo, I'm tired. I'm just really tired. I'm burning the candle at both ends." He described how every day, he'd leave his apartment before the sun was up and come home long after it set. He was balancing a heavy workload while also caring for his grandfather and mother at home.

I admire the heck out of Sam. Life has thrown more at him during the last decade than most of us will face in a lifetime. Through it all, Sam supported his family through sickness and sadness alike, put himself through college, balanced a promising career, and kept a strong interest in his friends' lives throughout it all. Sam is marked by a steady resolve, a fierce loyalty, and a gentleness only found in someone who's got nothing to prove.

As Sam trailed off, Mo picked up the conversation by adding what he'd been feeling, "Work, friends, family. There are a lot of different trees out there. I feel like more trees get planted as you get married, get a dog, change jobs. All that stuff as we get older."

Mo can be as quiet as Sam in a group setting but with just us, he was like the wiser older brother. He had always been one life step ahead of us. He could recount books, sermons, and experiences to point our conversation in a helpful direction no matter what our topic was. I used to follow Mo to the library in college. Hour after hour, he'd knock out practice finance exams and I'd try to keep up. I respected his grit. He also married his high-school sweetheart right after college. So, for two still-single guys, it felt like he spoke from a whole other realm of wisdom.

"Jeez," I thought. Sam's metaphor was spot on. Mo was right too.

This should be an easy metaphor to follow, even if you've never wielded an axe or used a handsaw to cut down a Christmas tree. Chopping down a tree is tiring. Without a chainsaw, you really have to work for every inch of progress, especially if you're hacking into a hard wood, like chestnut. When you think you're making some headway, you have to keep going until finally, the weight of the tree snaps the remaining splinters of wood.

As it crashes to the ground, you slump back in a combination of exhaustion and satisfaction, admiring how far you've come. Satisfaction soon turns into the sobering realization that axing one tree means you now have to do it 20 more times to apportion 10, two-foot logs for the fireplace. That realization gives way to exasperation as you look up at the rest of the trees in the forest that still need to be cut down.

———

Do you ever feel like your life is asking more of you today than it did yesterday? When was the last time you felt you were at a state of complete rest?

Incremental growth and success in my life has always brought more work and responsibility along with it. Just like a tree that falls, one accomplishment always melts into multiple, increasingly complex challenges. Some of those challenges are unavoidable, like more responsibility at work as my career progresses, and some of those challenges are self-assumed, like racing longer triathlons faster. In either case, as my story turns to a new chapter, I always find myself looking at a progressively demanding life and a crowded calendar.

Here's an example of what I mean. For most of us, success in our first job means managing people or assuming responsibility for their work in our second job. A stable and growing career means a paycheck to support a family. A family means a house, a house means repairs, mortgage payments, hosting holiday parties for out-of-town family, doing dishes, and... well, you get the picture. This idea of an escalating workload feels more familiar than foreign, regardless of where we come from.

The stories we're fed don't warn us about this workload. They hinge on characters who overcome adversity and endure hardship to find their happy ending. Because we don't see what happens after the final scene or the last chapter, we assume their life just gets easier from that day forward. Guy-saves-girl-from-certain-death and we assume they have a blissful, wonderful marriage in all chapters following. We don't see the long hours of spreading mulch, painting bathrooms, and dealing with the nosy neighbor who makes everyone else's business his business.

Our stories, on the other hand, will never be devoid of new and increasing challenges. Happily-ever-after will never look like coasting into the sunset for a life of ease and margaritas. There can be more than just burnout and weariness ahead of us, however. While there will always be some "tree to chop" in each new chapter of life, we can find rest amidst our life's work. It's possible to find restoration during our day-to-day struggles and the inevitable grind.

To find rest amidst unending work, we must look to our identity and how we derive our identity. There's an inseparable link between rest and identity. I discovered this after years of trying – and failing – to be both my story's author and lead character. Trying to create your own meaning and answering the big questions of your life (playing the author) while facing each day's little responsibilities (living as a character) is tiring.

———

"Nate, you can just 'be' sometimes, you know?" Brian (my co-founder and fellow entrepreneur) said as he poured me a glass of scotch and slid it across the table.

"Just sit down and stop for a while," he continued.

I looked up from my laptop, grabbing the glass. One month had passed since the night I ate tacos with Michael. It had been one week since I drank coffee with Sam and Mo. On this night, I found myself in a treehouse – an eco-home that someone rented out to travelers on Airbnb – thinking about the same themes of rest, work, and paradox.

"Be?" I asked, turning from my keyboard to my scotch.

"Yeah, you can just be Nate sometimes. You don't have to keep doing things. Just sit still and be for a while. It's good for you."

Brian is what you call an "empath." Not only does he have an uncanny level of self-awareness, he always knows what I need to hear. Empaths are a small subset of humans who have the natural, God-given ability to process, feel, and absorb another's emotions just because they're in the same room. Empaths don't necessarily need to know or be lifelong friends with someone. Proximity is enough to pick up on what they're feeling and, by extension, what they're thinking.

Brian's encouragement was part of why we were in a treehouse in the first place. We had kept up a sprint of projects all week long and by Friday morning, the city felt too suffocating to continue working. A mobile office in a random, remote Airbnb proved to be chicken soup for the soul – and our sanity – during weekend projects.

Of course I can just 'be.' I'm sitting still, aren't I? I thought to myself, but answered Brian, "Okay thanks. I'll try that."

I had missed the heart of what Brian was telling me. It went right over my head. As I considered Brian's directive, I was thinking that my "being" was simply contingent on the moment. If I was training, then I was a cyclist or a runner. If I was working, I was an entrepreneur (I liked that identity). If I was with family, I was a brother or a son. I was what I did, and I did a lot of things depending on the day.

Simply put, my activity defined me. I didn't think there was a way to "be" without doing.

Rarely was I just Nate. I'm not sure I could have even told you exactly who Nate was in that moment. Sure, I could have told you what he enjoyed, what projects he was working on, and what dreams he was chasing. Aside from listing off a string of growing accomplishments, however, I wasn't sure who I was at the very core of me.

I was insecurely overachieving my way into an epic story without stopping to examine the character I was becoming in the process. It's not like I was becoming a villain or an evil character. I was just running from one chapter to another (a theme in my story, you'll begin to notice) feeling anxious, tired, and strung out. There wasn't anything inherently wrong with that, so I simply pressed on.

"You cooked. Let me get the dishes tonight," I told Brian as I collected our plates.

Brian and I are good about being together without having to make conversation when we don't want it. I knew he'd be retiring to his room soon and I wanted to keep busy while thinking about why he would suggest I "just be." My gut reaction was to feel that yes, of course I could just be, but the more I thought about doing so, the more uncomfortable I felt.

Do you ever feel like you're falling behind?

Like there's a clock ticking and time is passing you by? And there's nothing you can do about it? That's exactly how I felt as I transitioned from the kitchen to my bedroom to just "be."

I sat on top of the sheets and looked at the silhouettes of the forest's trees tangoing with each other in the wind. I didn't feel that I was doing a good job of just being as I watched nature's moonlight dance. I felt an internal and unsettling commotion. My stillness only served to underscore the fact that I didn't much care for this feeling.

It's a concerning experience to feel a wave of anxiety rise up in you as a result of doing nothing more than sitting on your bed. I actually hope you can't relate to me here. You see, I was good at building a company, but I was terrible at building a meaningful story for myself. That night exposed me to the crushing reality that my activity defined me, so I lost my identity whenever I stopped moving or doing things.

I was pretending to be the author in all my pursuits. I had stopped looking to my Creator and how He had designed me to play a part of His greater, more meaningful story. I lost the context that gave my story consequence. I was only interested in pursuing my conquests. I thought that forward *motion* was what made me "me," and it created an inner *commotion* and an unsettled soul within me. I never stopped to look up at God or around at the story of our world.

———

I tried the same exercise of just sitting during a few different occasions over the next week. I'd ride home from our office, rack my bike, drop my bag, and plant myself on the carpet in the middle of the living room. I wouldn't even turn on the lights. I'd just sit cross-legged on the floor. By the third night of this, my floor-sitting began to make an impression. I found it was easier to avoid opening my phone and pulling the email screen down just to impatiently watch the cursor spin and reload.

The next morning, I practiced the same soul-stillness while I was in motion, riding my bike, waiting in line at the deli counter, or walking to grab coffee. I didn't listen to music. I didn't open my phone. I tried to just "be" as I went on throughout my day.

Prescribed, short interruptions to the hustle of my week began to force me into a greater sense of security. Essentially, I had to make myself hang out with myself for a little while. Isn't that odd? I realized that if it was hard for me to just be with myself for a few minutes, how excited could I really expect others to feel about hanging out with me?

Ultimately, practiced rest was helping me to reclaim who "Nate" had been created to be. By extension, just being Nate helped me to rest from the hard work of choppin' trees in an effort to achieve my way to an identity.

———

The following weekend, I was reminded of how we're able to rest easy if we choose to look to God as the Creator of our stories. We don't need to define ourselves by our activities (or any other means for that matter). I was told that despite the hard work and unending number of trees that life gives us to chop, we'll find rest if we trust there's someone greater narrating our story.

Jason Helveston, a Chicago pastor and author, was speaking during a church service on this particular morning. He's the type of preacher who makes you want to shake his hand and say, "Thanks, I needed that," after every sermon. He's refreshing. He creates the uncanny sensation he's speaking to you individually, even though you're sitting with scores of people in the audience.

"We value each other by how much we're needed. How busy, how tired we are. In fact, we fear what rest will cost us – our identity," Jason said to me (as I was seated in a crowd).

Woah. As he continued speaking, I set the back of my head on the top of my chair and looked up at the church's exposed ceiling. I rolled my head along the arc of the chair, side to side, hoping it would settle Jason's words into my soul. As they did, I saw how truth, yet again, showed up as a paradox.

When I stopped chasing my identity, I started to find it. Go figure, right? When I stopped pretending that I was powerful enough to work my way to an identity, I was free to find my identity as a character in God's Big Story.

Jason articulates this well when he says we often twist the script and confuse our role:

> [On one hand] Refusing to work idolizes comfort... [On the other hand] Working without the proper dose of rest inflates our self-worth and self-determinism because it binds us to a constant hustle that falsely promises our best life is right around the corner... In both temptations, we think we are God. And supposing ourselves to be divine kills us because, well, we are not divine. We are human beings... The remedy for all of this is Jesus... Jesus came to fill the void we daily try to fill with work and rest... he is the only one who could ever rightly say, "It is finished" (John 19:30).[iii]

It was not only exhausting to find my identity through my activity, I was actually pushing the core of who I am further and further away. My hustle had prevented me from understanding the inextricable, three-dimensional link between identity, work, and rest. Without being directed to look up to God and His design, I'd never have understood how there can be a symbiotic relationship between these three things.

————

There's this commercial where a guy walks around with a knife in his head and he only realizes that something's not right when a friend pulls the knife out. It's promoting a prescription migraine medication and the idea is that until the pain was removed, this poor fellow just assumed his pain was normal.

I can relate. In the four months preceding this chapter, I had woken up each morning with a weight pressing down on my chest. I hadn't known that was the case until it was gone. I'm not referring to a proverbial weight, either. Physically, I felt like I was being weighed down. I would wake up with this oppressive feeling that said if I had just "chopped down" so many trees yesterday, how could I possibly do it all over again? How was it that I'd wake up and start over, chopping my way out of a brand-new forest each day?

After Jason's sermon, I recognized I felt so oppressed because I was chasing something I'd never catch. A chase without an ending is exhausting. A race with no finish line is madness. I had been trying to cultivate an identity through productivity and work and output when the reality is that around the corner of finished work is just more work that needs to be done.

Finding rest and capturing my identity was never going to come at the end of a to-do list. As I'd approach the finish line to one project, I'd open the door to three or four more. It will always be that way, too. Slowly, I awoke to the truth that rest can come in the middle of our work if we trust that our identities aren't found in or through our work.

Resting while working. It's backward, I know.

I wanted to study what others had to say on the topic so I started reading more. I went back to an old favorite, C.S. Lewis'

Mere Christianity. To this day, I have this quote saved in my phone to remind me:

> It comes the very moment you wake up each morning. All your wishes and hopes for the day rush at you like wild animals. And the first job each morning consists simply in shoving them all back; in listening to that other voice, taking that other point of view, letting that other larger, stronger, quieter life come flowing in. And so on, all day. Standing back from all your natural fussings and frettings; coming in out of the wind.[iv]

I started articulating my newfound thoughts to another good friend, Kyle. I met Kyle at a football game a few years prior. I had been talking to someone about the University of Illinois and Kyle turned around from the row in front of me to say, "Hey, I'm an Illini, you too?" Soon after that, he gave me a room in his apartment. I met his roommate JP (who later introduced me to my future wife), and Kyle coached me through almost every major life decision from then on out.

Kyle is brilliant enough to beat a computer in a game of chess, but he's also cool enough to have spent a few days trekking through the Amazon jungle with me. He sees angles I don't. He's always interested in answering my questions, too, so I asked him out to dinner to get his input on what I'd been learning.

We met for barbecue after a few more weeks of my cross-legged floor-sitting. Ever since the summer I moved into Kyle's apartment, we seemed to connect over barbecue. While we'd wait for our food, I'd try to stump him with a brainteaser (and fail most times). That night, however, we didn't swap riddles. I just got right down to explaining the weight I had felt pressing down on me every morning.

I dragged my sweet potato fries through small ponds of honey, listening to Kyle tell me, "You should try speaking while you're just sitting. It brings you back to the moment. It untangles twisted thoughts. It's what I do."

"Really? You can relate?" I couldn't believe it. I asked him again to make sure that I was following. "You mean you need to do this stuff, too?"

"Yeah, I just talk about what's happening around me. Like, what time is it? What are you wearing? What's your name? That kind of stuff. 'I'm Kyle. I'm wearing a blue striped shirt, and I'm eating sweet potato fries and honey with Nate.'"

He continued, "It sounds strange until you actually do it. But when you do, it's hard to forget who you are and where you are in the present moment."

———

I found another perspective on my work, rest, and identity crisis in an email newsletter that week. Seth Godin is a bald marketing whiz who turns big concepts into simple sentences with practical advice – all delivered via email. I read about the opposite extreme of the work-rest balance as I scrolled through my email drinking coffee and eating peanut-butter toast.

Mr. Godin wrote about how to avoid journeying too far into apathy. He said we often recoil from responsibility altogether when we feel burnt-out or when we over-personalize our work. Our instinct is to rid ourselves of work completely in order to find rest. To continue the analogy, the thinking is that if I don't finish chopping down this tree, then I don't have to move onto that one, right?

That's cheap rest, however, and refusing to play the role written for you isn't satisfying. Mr. Godin's email said:

> To walk lightly through the world, with confidence and energy, is far more compelling than plodding along, worn down by the weight on your shoulders. It might be tempting to try to relieve yourself of responsibility, but it's a downward spiral... Better, I think, to learn to dance with it. To take it seriously, not personally.[v]

The work isn't personal – it's not our identity. We're free to take our work seriously without allowing it to define us.

———

This ebb and flow of work and rest has been written into all our stories. Our Creator wanted it that way. Once we've been created, we don't have to keep working to build ourselves up. If we want to uncover more meaning in our ordinary days, we just need to look to our Creator to understand our true purpose.

When I discovered that my work flows out of my identity – it's not the path to creating my identity – I no longer despaired when I couldn't finish or get past the work. I found rest while chopping down the trees life sprang up (and will continue to spring forth). I didn't have to fear rest. I was no longer falling behind by just "being" for a few moments.

Life became like cake for me.

A cake just sits in the oven and it changes so slowly you wouldn't even notice. But, if you looked at its doughy beginning, walked away, and then looked at the end result, you'd think it came from something totally different than dough. While it will indeed look and taste different, we know dough didn't achieve its cake status on its own. The oven and the baker, its creators, did the heavy lifting. The dough simply played its part to become cake.

I don't know if God likes cake, but I think he agrees with this idea of finding rest amidst our work. He even sent his Son to say a few words to us on the topic: *"Take My yoke upon you and learn from Me, for I am gentle and humble in heart, and you will find rest for your souls... For My yoke is easy and My burden is light."*[vi]

I try to live with this in mind. To this day, I leave my phone in the car or switched off during dinner with friends or family.

Each morning, I sit cross-legged on the couch to prevent myself from rushing into the day. If it's been a particularly long week, I close my laptop early on Friday afternoons. I don't bring a phone charger on short trips; I've missed what's happening around me if I've used my phone that much.

Do you have a certain practice or habit that reminds you to rest? Do you need one?

Surprises & Sunrises

August 2015

- extraordinary moments are found in everyday settings -

*There is wonder in our ordinary and everyday surroundings,
like sunrises and stars. However, I wouldn't have noticed
until I stopped moving, or more accurately, until I had
someone point it out to me through a photo.*

E ach chapter always build on the chapters that came before it. The best stories are arranged with intention and in a precise order because characters, setting, and plot don't create good stories by themselves. These elements must develop with purpose as the story progresses. Looking back, I see that my life story has worked in the exact same way. While at some points I feel I'm regressing to relearn the same lessons for a second time, each of my life's chapters has always prepared me to embrace the events that will unfold in the next chapter.

At this point, it was important that the weighted-down feelings started to leave me. I was going to meet a new character

– a girl – during this next chapter of my story. Now that I was healthier emotionally, I was free to start looking around me instead of focusing on the endless work in front of me. Healthy relationships are formed by two individually-healthy people, so finding work-rest balance in my life was an important first step.

Her name was (and is) Erin. She came as a surprise to me. I wasn't looking to date anyone, but once I started seeing her, my story about ambition and big goals quickly became a love story.

I wouldn't have arrived at someone as perfect as Erin if it was my place to design the girl I'd eventually marry. I think I would have created someone like me, but Erin is very different from me. Erin's roommate, Tiffany, called me out on this once. She said, "You know Nate, Erin's not just a weird guy. She's a woman. She's entirely different, not just a different version of you." That's a good thing, too. I've learned more from Erin than I ever expected and it all started the first time I saw her watching the sun rise.

––––––

Erin can find big joy in small things.

I noticed this during our first week of hanging out in a series of what Erin calls our "non-date dates." While I wasn't looking to date anyone (I hadn't gone out on a date in three years at this point), I changed my mind rather quickly when I saw her marveling at an early morning sunrise over Lake Michigan.

As Erin knelt on Ohio Street Beach taking pictures of the sun's colors crawling over the horizon, it dawned on me that something was different about her. I realized that Erin has a rare, instinctive ability to see the extraordinary in ordinary settings.

But wait, why were we at the beach? Six months before that sunrise, we were both attending an engagement party for one of my past roommates, JP, who I lived with when Kyle took me in. JP is one of Erin's childhood friends. Erin and I ended up closing down that engagement party, sitting on the couch talking for hours about how she was training for the Chicago Marathon.

Despite having a great conversation and forgetting I was in the middle of another party, I never followed up with her. I was oblivious to the strong possibility that Erin had only talked about endurance sports for three hours because I liked sports – and she liked me. I missed the sign. Most guys would have asked her out right then and there. But me? I waited six months before randomly forwarding her an email with a registration link for the Chicago Triathlon that said three words, "Wanna sign up?"

That's it. Not, "Hey, remember me? I've been thinking about you..." Romantic, I know. After Erin read my email, she replied she'd only sign up if I agreed to teach her to swim in the open water with a wetsuit. I like early mornings and pretty girls, so I figured that was a good deal. We began meeting every Wednesday at 6 a.m. at Ohio Street Beach for swim lessons in the bone-chilling waters of Lake Michigan.

———

Erin realized I was standing near the beachside lockers. She turned around and ran up from the water's edge, yelling out, "Morning! Don't you just love sunrises?!"

I laughed as I pulled my wetsuit from my backpack. I had been at the beach for a few minutes, leaning against my bike and watching her watch the sunrise. We see the exact same sun rise and set every day, and we know the precise time it will return the next day. Yet, she was enthralled by today's sunrise in particular.

She turned her phone toward me and scrolled through each of the different pictures. She explained why she liked them, "In this one, you can see the sun's rays cutting in different directions over the line of the pier. But in this one, you can see how the sun's color reflects in the water, and how the horizon cuts the photo across the top. Pretty cool, right?"

I had to admit, they were very cool. Just as cool was how Erin could find new ways to look at the same sun simply because it was a new day. I noticed her smile and curious brown eyes. She became even more beautiful when captivated by something that was exciting to her, like sunrises. I wasn't sure what to look at – Erin, the photos, or the sunrise – so I just smiled and took the phone to flip through more pictures.

"Woah. These are really good, Erin. You should frame some of these. Have you printed them before?"

"Yeah, but just for family or sometimes friends. I'd like for people to buy them for their homes one day, but people don't really buy pictures of things and places. People like portraits of themselves, or of their kids, more than they like sunrises." She shrugged.

"Oh." I shrugged too and turned toward the water.

"So, the water's pretty cold today, 59 degrees as of last night. You ready for this?" I asked, stuffing my backpack into one of the public lockers.

"I kinda have to be, don't I?" Erin confessed, setting her Contigo mug of morning coffee into my locker.

"You'll be okay. Your body numbs after the first shock of cold. It'll be coldest on your face but you'll be fine once it passes," I said, unsure of how reassuring my words actually were.

I slipped my wetsuit over my ankles, worked it up to my waist, and stretched it over my shoulders. I watched Erin do the same, laughing quietly as she sat back on the sand, out of breath and struggling with the rear zipper. I knelt and zipped up her suit before we waded into the water to adjust to the icy temperatures.

If you're wondering, I now know that a girl must be into you if she's willing to yank on a skin-tight wetsuit, ditch the makeup, and stretch a swim cap over her hair for a first non-date date. I didn't know that at the time, however, so much of this chapter is about me catching up to what's developing in my own story.

———

Thirty minutes later, which feels like an eternity in icy water, we were stripping off our wetsuits and pulling on our running shoes. The deal was that after each swim session, we'd fit in Erin's scheduled marathon training before the workday started.

I liked the running portion of our mornings. It was a good time to ask questions without feeling too investigative. We weren't sitting across from each other, like during a dinner date, so deeper questions felt a little more relaxed. Plus, if we were setting a hard pace, we both welcomed the distraction.

With my license for curiosity I asked Erin, "Why do you like looking at the sunrise?"

"Well, I guess sunrises reminds me of good things," she said. "They remind me of sitting near the water in Lake Geneva on summer mornings. I like it there. You should meet my friends who live there, I think you'd like them too. Oh, and I like new days. A sunrise means it's a new day. Sometimes I can't stay in bed, even if I'm tired just because I see the sun in my window."

I started to say something in agreement, but then she continued, "And you know, they're always different. Yesterday's sunrise was different from today's, so there's always something new to look at. It's like art in the sky, you know?"

"Yeah..." I managed to mumble before Erin jumped in.

"If only I had a camera that could really capture the sunrise. Like, show it to you in the same way you see it when you're sitting near the water. I don't know if a picture will ever look as good as the real thing, though."

Apparently, I had asked the right question. Sunrises meant something to her. Strangely, I realized that meant something to me too. I was definitely open to more runs with a pretty girl who came alive with good questions and sunrises. It was easier than I thought it would be, talking with Erin. She just seemed to get it. She shared my general curiosity for life.

———

It was week three of swimming with Erin. We stopped just short of the beachside lockers on the way back from our run.

"Next Wednesday?" I confirmed.

"Yep, but you're missing one thing this week." Erin clicked her locker open and pulled out a brown, brand new Contigo mug (a mug you can easily bike with because the top has a little button to open and close the mouth piece).

"I got this for you." Erin extended her arm toward me, placing the mug in my hand. She looked away slightly, dipping her shoulders down and shifting her feet, nervously waiting to hear my reaction.

"Erin, this is awesome, and really thoughtful. Thank you," I said as I tucked it into my backpack and smiled.

Later that night, I found a small square printout tucked inside the mug. I smiled as I pulled it out. She had printed a photo of the sun rising over Ohio Street Beach with a blue hue and a caption that said "Tri-City."

———

There is wonder in our ordinary and everyday surroundings, like sunrises and stars. However, I wouldn't have noticed until I stopped moving, or more accurately, had someone point it out to me through a photo. I think we're blinded to the wonder in our daily lives for two reasons. The first reason is motion; we're always on the go and seldom do we sit still long enough to see the extraordinary. The second reason is "proximity;" trivial things distract and divert our attention.

From the last chapters, it's clear I had learned much about the balance of work, rest, and just "being." However, before that morning on Ohio Street Beach, I hadn't considered that the ability to find wonder in everyday settings is yet another dimension to rest and stillness. GK Chesterton illustrates this as he talks about how incessant, ceaseless motion is a barrier to wonder by using moss – the green stuff that grows on trees – as an example:

> In the heated idleness of youth we were all rather inclined to quarrel with the implication of that proverb which says that a

rolling stone gathers no moss. We were inclined to ask, "Who wants to gather moss, except silly old ladies?" But for all that we begin to perceive the proverb is right. The rolling stone rolls echoing from rock to rock; but the rolling stone is dead. The moss is silent because the moss is alive.[vii]

Ordinary days felt oppressive to me. They made me feel like I was falling behind. Like I was losing or becoming a more-hollow person if I didn't see or experience something new. That feeling forced me to move just for the sake of moving. Yet, like moss growing on a rock, there is life in the stillness that comes with a normal day. The longer the rock sits, the thicker and greener the moss grows. The more alive it becomes. Should that rock roll and tumble down the valley, the moss loses that same life.

The second barrier to wonder is proximity, and it's so ubiquitous and pervasive in modern life that we rarely stop to consider it. Nathan Rittenhouse, an expert in "meta-narratives" (the philosophical study of how we interpret circumstances and patterns to create an overarching structure for our beliefs, values, and meaning), explains proximity like this:

> We simply cannot see into the heavens because of all the light that is constantly around us. Very few of us are ever in total darkness because there is always a light somewhere nearby or in our pocket. This is all a bit silly. Just think, there are thousands of visible stars above my head that are incomprehensibly bright, and yet, I cannot see them because of a streetlamp 18-feet above my head that is a negligible fraction

of a single star's brilliance. There is a world of untold splendor twinkling above my head that the ancients stared into for years, and yet I can't see the reflection of this beauty because of the dim glow of my phone. My inability to see this beauty is not a problem with the brilliance of their lights; rather it is the problem of my proximity to lesser lights.[viii]

Each barrier is conflated into a deadly stranglehold on our attention. The motion of our lives' productivity, conquest, and ever-connectedness keeps us fretting and forgetting to be still. We're unable to fathom that something far more brilliant lies beyond the lesser lights surrounding us.

———

As I sat looking at the picture Erin had rolled up inside of my new mug, I began to understand how we can experience our lives' most extraordinary moments by simply being present enough to spot them as they appear in everyday surroundings. With a little help from Erin smiling at a sunrise, I was still building on what Greg showed me while eating watermelons in Costa Rica, and what Brian reinforced while handing me a glass of scotch in a little tree house.

How to Safety-Pin a Memory

September 2015

- simple gestures carry the most significant meaning -

*Erin explained that her heart had swelled during a moment I
once found immaterial enough to forget. She had filed away the
feeling of me attaching a safety pin.*

———————

"Oh great, I go to Brazil and I'm replaced!" Daniel cried into
the phone and snapped his fingers, "Just like that!"

Daniel was partly joking, but he was also serious. He was
working for an international consulting firm and he had been
assigned to a multi-month project in Brazil. While he was living
in São Paulo, getting crushed by 100-hour workweeks, I had
given him a call to say that I started swimming again. This time,
however, I was swimming with a girl. Swimming had been our
thing, you see. For years we'd wake each other up for early
morning training sessions. We traveled to different states and
countries racing together.

"No, no, no. Nobody can replace you. It's different," I started to explain before Daniel jumped in.

"I'm hangin' by a thread! I'm reading don't-kill-myself books here, and you're telling me you're getting married!"

He was quoting one of our favorite movies, *Wedding Crashers*. Daniel's a treasure trove of movie quotes. I'm fairly certain he could fill a whole day of completely normal conversation while only speaking in movie quotes.

"Just tell me when the wedding is."

"You better get your ass to that wedding," I matched his quote.

I didn't realize it at the time but there was foreshadowing behind my words. Erin and I had only been swimming together for a few weeks, but she was already waiting for me to take her out on a real date. I told myself I'd wait to ask her out until after our triathlon and her Chicago Marathon. I didn't want to become an awkward distraction in the event she said no.

———

"Dude, what happened? Where have you been?" I asked, not sure if I should laugh or be concerned.

It was the morning of the Chicago Triathlon, for which Erin and I had been training. My buddy, Travis, had also signed up to race with us, but the race organizers were beginning to tear down the check-in table and there was no sign of him anywhere.

I tried his cell phone. No answer. Erin and I were growing pretty anxious, wondering if he would arrive with enough time to pick up his race number.

Then, Travis appeared, rolling his bike toward the check-in area. "So... funny story. I was putting my bike together late last night, which was my first mistake, and I noticed my rear tire was flat. I had to figure something out, and the bike shops near me were all closed, so I went to a CVS and picked up some super glue and cloth patches. I figured, heck, that's a bike patch, right?"

Travis laughed, which was relieving. If he was laughing at the situation then we could too.

"So, I did that, and it worked, but it must have lost some air overnight and I didn't notice until I was riding here. I pedaled slowly, so I think I should be good-to-go. I'll just pump more air into it before we check our gear at the transition zone. All good!"

I shook my head, still laughing. The scene perfectly captured Travis' carefree approach to life. I turned to check on Erin and saw her relax as she chatted with Travis. She had a case of the pre-race jitters. Travis is livelier than a hummingbird on a sugar rush so he matched her nervous energy and conversation with ease. I felt how I always feel on race morning – even-tempered, no nerves, no excitement. I was just ready to race.

Small raindrops fell as we walked through Grant Park. I smiled, recalling the familiar sensation of rain drops on race morning. I glanced at the sun creeping over the horizon. I thought about Erin's photos of the sun rising over Ohio Street Beach that one morning. As we walked, I saw her gaze was fixed on the sun's faint rays poking through grey clouds.

We approached the makeshift transition zone constructed on the south side of Grant Park. Athletes were hanging their bikes along rows of racks, pumping tires, zipping wetsuits, and laying out their run gear before hustling back to the north side of the park. There, everyone clustered themselves according to the color of their swim cap and waited for their turn to dive into the frigid waters of Lake Michigan.

Laying out your gear in a transition zone is the most stressful part of a triathlon. It's when your pre-race excitement mixes with your nerves, and you pray you didn't forget anything important as you lay out your equipment around your bike leaving enough time to return to the start line. There are a lot of logistics inherent to combining three separate sports into one event. It's especially easy to feel frazzled if it's your first race. And, when you multiply three sports by hundreds of athletes, that's a whole lot of gear in the same place.

I had raced in the Triathlon World Championships in Sweden a few months before this, so by comparison, this race was a walk in the park. Figuring out how to re-build your bike from an airplane case, follow the USA Trainer's rules and team schedule, and mentally prepare to race over 100 miles is just on a totally different level than a for-fun, 18-mile race. So, I breezed through my mental checklist, set up my gear, and wandered up the rows of bikes to find Erin.

I spotted her in the maze of people with her bike and run gear organized, wetsuit zipped. She was ready, and I was duly impressed. I yanked my wetsuit over my shoulders and dropped a safety pin I was holding between my lips into my hand. I held it up for Erin to see before kneeling down to her feet. I didn't think about explaining what I was doing; I just reached for the timing chip attached to her neoprene ankle strap and looped the safety pin around the Velcro portion, ensuring it wouldn't unfasten during the race.

In a triathlon, every athlete is given a timing chip on a Velcro strap to track his or her time. Different from 5Ks, marathons, or other single-sport events, you have to wear a wetsuit and change your shoes. So, you secure your timing chip to an ankle strap instead of your jersey or shoes. However, stripping off a skin-tight wetsuit in a hurry can easily rip off the Velcro.

"There," I said, standing back up. "All secure."

"Thanks, I wouldn't have thought of that," Erin smiled as we walked to the start line.

———

I discovered that Erin was into me one month after our triathlon. It required several friends pointing out the obvious to me. Somehow, it never crossed my mind that Erin had been dunking herself into cold water in the wee hours of the morning out of true love, not just a love for triathlon. Once I crawled out from underneath my rock of oblivion, I asked her out on a proper date-date.

She said yes, and after that, we didn't need the excuse of training for a race to see each other. No more non-date dates for us. We let our swim-dates become dinner-dates. After three weeks of nights spent wandering the city, lingering in restaurant booths, and even traveling to my family's farm in Southern Illinois, I was fairly confident that she not only liked me, but that she'd also be open to dating me. There's a difference between going out on dates and dating, you see. There's intention and a small commitment that accompanies a label.

We decided to take a walk along the 606 – an old Chicago train track that was converted into a bike and pedestrian path – one Sunday afternoon. Though I hadn't planned it this way, an urban trail lined with flowers would communicate the right balance of romanticism while asking Erin to be my girlfriend. I figured that asking while we were out for another swim or bike ride just wouldn't convey the true sincerity with which I wanted to ask.

After we had been walking for a few minutes, I decided it was time. I turned to Erin and asked, "What do you need to know about me to move from going out on dates, to dating?"

Erin smiled as she replied, "Nothing, Nate. You know, had you asked me out two years ago, I'd have said yes then too."

I turned to her, confused.

"Yeah, I've been waiting for this day."

"Waiting? As in, you knew this was coming?"

"Not exactly, but after the first day I met you, I came home and told Tiffany about you. We talked about you all the time, and I'd just get so nervous whenever I ran into you. You never noticed?"

"No! Definitely not. I couldn't figure you out."

"Well it's true. I never could have asked you out though. You always needed to ask me. You knew when the timing was right." Erin had been patient. She knew good stories build over time.

I didn't want our day to end so my solution was to ask her the brilliant question, "Tacos? How do those sound?" It sounded much better in my head. She probably just thought I was hungry.

"Sure!" Erin said, understanding I wanted to spend more time together. She hears the things I don't say. It's one of the reasons we work so well together.

We sat down in a corner booth in a cozy, family-run Mexican restaurant a few blocks from her apartment. While we got our money's worth of free tortilla chips and salsa, I wondered what else I didn't know about her.

"So, you've been ahead of me this whole time. What else do I need to catch up on?" I asked, scooping another chip full of salsa. Erin consumes tortilla chips faster than the average person, so I was doing my best to keep up. As she walked me through the conversations she used to have about me with Tiffany, her mom, and her friends, she lost me when she mentioned our triathlon.

"…and that time you safety-pinned my timing chip before our race…"

I stopped her. "Wait, you noticed that? That was special?"

I couldn't deduce why she'd list a safety pin among our most memorable moments. Out of all the moments in a day as thrilling as race day – let alone all the hours we spent training and watching sunrises together – a safety pin was among the most significant.

"Of course!" Erin exclaimed. The memory was so clear to her. "I didn't ask you to help me, but you were looking out for me. You had a race to focus on, and you really love racing, yet you were thinking of how my race would go. So, you just knelt down at my feet and made sure I was going to be okay."

I remembered wrapping Erin in a bear hug at the race's finish line. I recalled the thrill of dancing with her on my rooftop, overlooking the city's midnight skyline. I felt my racing heart beat as we climbed into a fenced-off park to watch Navy Pier's Ferris Wheel in the moonlight. These were the big moments of our non-date-dates. Nevertheless, Erin's heart swelled during a moment I once found immaterial enough to forget. She filed away the feeling of me attaching a safety pin while I may never have remembered those five seconds.

Looking back, I now see that meaning showed up on race day through another paradox; the simplest gestures carry the most significant meaning. What seemed insignificant to me carried great weight for Erin.

How I communicated that Erin was valuable to me depended on her story's history. I had to understand her context before I could appreciate what words, moments, and interactions were significant to her. A safety pin represented security to Erin, which was entirely consistent with the memories she had shared while we jogged along the lakeshore.

The first memory Erin shared with me was about her older brother, Ryan, and how she always knew he was her protector. Ryan is eight years older, wiser, and has this ever-sharp awareness of what's happening around him. He willingly signs up to serve as the designated driver. He's prepared with a knife and flashlight whenever needed. He kept Erin safe as she played in their front yard as a kid, and she always knew she didn't have to worry if her big brother was around.

Erin's mom, Kathy, also represented security growing up. Kathy would work long, tiring days and even nights to make sure Erin never wanted for anything. When her mom was away at work, Erin would turn on the TV while she waited for her to come home. She loved seeing her mom walk into the house on those nights, and I can say now, having married Erin, nothing's changed. When I walk into our bedroom after a late-night flight, I find her asleep on our bed with Netflix rolling along on her laptop. The lights and sounds remind her of waiting to see her mom walk into the living room.

So, while most people were thinking about their own race goals, mumbling about the cold rain, or hustling to the start line, I was cemented in Erin's memory because I took the time to make her feel secure. It was just part of a routine for me, but it meant the world to her – all because of the world from which she comes. It was the perfect example of how I speed through my routines and as a result, I blow past the meaning underlying short interactions and simple gestures.

I think we all safety-pin certain memories, just like Erin. Our personal stories are created by the experiences we've filed away according to their importance to us, even if they appear inconsequential to someone else. At the time, I believed my story was about a guy who was running head-first through life. I was chasing my dreams of building a company and racing fast triathlons. Erin knew that life can be much more meaningful than that, however.

She understood that good stories are written about people and relationships. As a result, she caught the significance in a simple moment when I didn't stop to see it.

Do you have a favorite "safety-pinned" memory? If so, why is it important to you? If someone else played a meaningful role in that memory, do they know it?

Nike Sign

- the biggest goals are achieved by the smallest steps -

I thought big breakthroughs would just keep happening to me.
I thought I'd just wait for it and then suddenly, the chance to quit
my job and run off to a great new adventure would smack me in
the face. That happened to me once. When it didn't keep
happening, I grew impatient.

———————

It had taken more than two years for the greatest part of my life, my relationship with Erin, to move from first conversation to first date. Similarly, 18 months would pass before we moved from first date to wedding date. I think this is why we always talk about "growing" relationships or "building" reputations; good things take time.

Relationally, this made sense to me. It was easy to appreciate how multiple months and the preceding seasons had readied us for a healthy, thriving relationship. However, I hadn't yet applied this idea – that small, slow, intentional steps develop into the most meaningful parts of our stories over time – to other areas of my life. Naturally, that's where our next chapter begins.

Have you ever held a conversation that goes like this?

Question: "How'd you do that? Show me how."

Response: "Well, I don't know. You just do it."

Questioner: "What do you mean you 'just do it?'"

Responder: "Yeah, you just do it!"

It's as unhelpful an exchange as it is accurate. Although not very instructive, whether we're talking about asking for a promotion or jumping from a cliff into water, the difference between doing something and not doing something is often just *doing it.* Intention is a good starting point, but it's not the same as action. Small and seemingly inconsequential steps repeated over and over again always produce the most fulfilling endings.

———

"Glad I don't wear a suit every day," I grumbled to myself.

It was hot for November. As I rode my bike in a grey patterned suit, I tried to avoid sweating through my suit jacket while simultaneously avoiding black, greasy smudges on my pants. It wasn't a fun ride. Besides, wearing a suit generally means you're in for small talk. I'd rather peel potatoes with a plastic spoon than make conversation over cocktails with people I don't know.

On this particular occasion, I was in fact headed to an evening of small talk. I was planning to meet Brian at a networking event for nonprofit consultants in Chicago. At the time, our company's platform helped small nonprofits increase funding for their programs by matching them with consultants who had extra, unbilled hours of time. We were growing quickly and we needed to hire more consultants. Thus, networking was part of the job.

Most people don't realize that raising money for nonprofits is an actual, professional career. So, I'll give you some context. I'm wholly stereotyping, but walking into a room of fundraising consultants requires mentally preparing yourself to smile at hours of grandstanding and parading. Conversations largely consist of one-upping someone else's accomplishments to make your own career appear more successful. Many are much more down-to-earth than that, but fundraising conferences are often just a place to air out your own awesomeness.

Sounds like a fun night, right?

I met Brian in one of Chicago's main restaurant districts and we took our time ambling down the street. I wasn't sure if it was the heat, or if neither of us were particularly interested in attending the event, but we were moving at a glacial pace. I followed three steps behind Brian, partly to roll my bike along the sidewalk's edge, but mostly to give us enough time to find an escape route. We all but slowed to a stop as we approached a well-regarded sushi restaurant. Brian loves sushi.

"So… this should be fun. I'm hungry, though. How 'bout you?" Brian inquired.

"Definitely. Sushi?" I pointed to the bold red lettering across the street.

"Sounds great," he nodded as we picked up our pace.

"Way to come through in the clutch, sushi," I thought in quiet triumph.

Our subtle exchange was code for skipping the event. Food would be served at the event so by going out to eat before, we were really saying we'd cut ourselves some slack. We'd hang out, eat sushi, drink, and it would be close enough to the end of the event that we'd call it a night. It had been too long a week and too brutal a day to work up the energy for smiling, shaking hands, and listening to people drone on about how amazing they are.

"G'evening gentlemen, can I get you two some drinks?" our waitress asked as we settled into high-backed chairs at the bar.

"Double Bombay Sapphire martini, up, three blue-cheese olives, please." Brian didn't hesitate; he knew what he wanted. Maybe it was what he needed. I wasn't sure, but I ordered a beer.

"Do you ever feel that building a company shouldn't be this hard? Like, we have the vision, we know it'll work out, so why can't we make more progress each day?" I bemoaned while we waited for our much-needed drinks to arrive.

"Yes, but I can't think like that. I couldn't do this job if I did. It's too hard to even consider," he sighed.

"Okay fellas, are you thinking food, too?" Our waitress set down our drinks and turned the skewer of olives toward Brian.

"Oh yes, yes," Brian said. "Bring us five rolls, your choice, you plan the menu. Whatever you like the most."

She smiled, excited by the idea. I lifted my beer and thought that Brian, intentionally or unintentionally, had just livened up her night. He interrupted the repetition of just taking and punching in orders all night long.

"I guess we don't see the totality of everything we just show up and do at the office every day. Not until we have a year to look back on, at least," I said.

"Yeah, we don't really notice slow progress. But it doesn't mean we're not making progress."

Pessimism was the subtle danger that threatened to creep up and undermine our work if we didn't defend against it. Amidst long hours of showing up day after day to do the work that wasn't fun, but necessary nonetheless, we rarely took the time to reflect on what was developing. Each day, we'd only make incremental headway from the previous day. We even lost ground on some days. But, we were actually leaps and bounds ahead of where we'd been at the same time the year prior.

"I used to believe businesses are built by brilliant ideas and earth-shattering moments. I know better now," Brian laughed.

"It's almost like the bigger your vision, the more phone calls you answer, checks you write, and emails you send. Nothing gets done if we don't just do that stuff." I agreed.

"Yep. We are the sum of several little jobs."

———

I used to think big breakthroughs would keep happening to me. I thought I'd just wait for it and then suddenly, the chance to quit my job and run off to a grand new adventure would smack me in the face. That happened to me once. I grew impatient when it didn't keep happening. It took beer and sushi while ditching a networking event to help me realize that that kind of big-idea thinking is far from reality.

Good things are sketched out slowly by the drudgery of everyday life. As funny as it sounds, just showing up and doing the little things really well is the "big idea." In almost every area of life, little things become big things with a lot of effort. It's those big things built by little things that are most meaningful over the long run.

———

Monuments show up throughout the stories preserved in the Bible. Sometimes, monuments helped the nation of Israel to remember the lessons that they, like us, needed to relearn time and time again. On other occasions, monuments displayed just how far and faithfully God had guided them throughout history.

There's a story in the Bible about one of Israel's leaders named Joshua. It says God instructed him, "Tell one man from each of the twelve tribes [of Israel] to pick up a large rock from where the priests are standing. Then have the men set up those rocks as a monument at the place where you camp tonight."[ix]

Joshua told the guys picking up the rocks, "Someday your children will ask, 'Why are these rocks here?' Then you can tell them how the water stopped flowing when the chest was being carried across the river. These rocks will always remind our people of what happened here today."[x]

God knows we need reminders (a lot of them) to make lessons stick, but our monuments look a little different these days. Photos, scrapbooks, and picture frames are all more practical than having a bunch of rocks lying around. I decided after Brian and I ate sushi that we, too, needed a monument in our office. We needed a reminder that companies, relationships, and reputations don't just happen. They're built slowly and daily.

We had just sent out an end-of-year update to the network of consultants we contracted with through our platform. It recapped the progress we'd made throughout the past year, and it previewed our goals for the year ahead. We had distributed a similarly themed email the prior year, so I sent a file of each to our graphic designer, Reid, and asked him, "Can you put these emails side by side? As a mural with an arrow arcing up from last year's short list of achievements, to this year's long list?"

I took Reid's design and printed it onto 60-inch poster board. Blown up and side by side, the progress was encouraging. It was like looking at two different companies. I hung it near Brian's desk to remind us that in the tiring, ordinary moments of office life, we were actually on the road to building something of lasting consequence.

Do you have any monuments in your life? If not, do you need to create one for a certain lesson or part of your story?

———

That same month, another company, based in Washington D.C., initiated talks of merging our services with theirs. They created software for nonprofits, and we created strategies through services from a network of consultants. So, the two offerings complemented each other very well. As I ran into the office with a backpack full of clothes one morning, I considered what might happen if the merger-talks escalated.

The added weight of my backpack slowed me from my usual pace. I used the reduced tempo to let my mind speed up. I wondered what life in the new company's headquarters would be like, if we even ended up there. I didn't have a crystal ball and

I desperately wanted to forecast how the next few months would transpire. "If only I could look forward and then arrange my present days accordingly, life would be better," I thought.

I was craving the confidence of knowing what, if anything, would come of the acquisition talks. Would we move to D.C.? I hadn't thought about proposing to Erin yet, so would she visit me there? Would we be able to make it while dating long-distance? As I sauntered onward, I yanked my backpack straps tight in frustration. It was useless. This was one part of my life that was clearly so far beyond my control that asking more questions wouldn't equal more certainty.

I cut underneath a set of train tracks and continued up a steep incline on Kinzie Street. As I carried on, I contemplated how I was pressing forward despite my inability to see what lay beyond the hill's crest. Knowing what waited at the top wouldn't have helped me put one foot in front of the other. Yet, I craved a similar knowledge in my professional and personal life. Even though we'll never know how our chapters end when we're living in the middle of them, I wanted to read from the manuscript we're able to piece together after living forward and then looking backward.

In that moment, the best advice was for me to "just do it," welcoming the maturity I'd gain by enduring the uncertainty. I needed to move ahead without the luxury of a clear-cut path.

Did you know that paintings rarely turn out like they do in the artist's head before getting started? Paintings, music, books, and all forms of art change with each small brush, note, or keystroke. The artist learns from the patterns and paint already imprinted on the canvas, and from there, he or she knows how to shade the next stroke a bit differently.

In the same way, if it were possible to just will our complete life story into existence at once, fathoming the complete events of our lives in a single instance, it would never turn out as satisfying as we had hoped. God already designed a far more beautiful story than anything we could construct. The present moment is our chance to savor it. Over time, if we continue to "just do it" and move forward, we'll be able to look back and see how all things worked together to form something far superior to anything we'd have orchestrated.

As I made my way across the Chicago River, I thought of a proverb: "Many are the plans in the mind of a man, but it is the purpose of the Lord that will stand." It slowed me to a walk. I paid more attention to my thoughts than to my legs as I muttered softly, "I'm pretty arrogant, aren't I?"

I still wanted to be the author of my life. I longed to control my future, and I craved the foreknowledge that being my own creator would afford. My pride had tricked me into attempting to map out my own game plan for my life, instead of trusting God to work out His plan.

I picked up my pace. I thought about how the belief that faith is something that allows us to sit around, waiting for everything to work out, is actually way off base. I realized I had a call to action – a call to live with a "just do it" mentality – knowing that if I did so, God would shape the outcome along the way.

———

Years before this, a friend had given me a small cardboard square with a quote from Tony Robbins printed on it. It was sitting on a bookshelf in my office when I walked in from my run. While Mr. Robbins' worldview misses the mark (in my opinion) and he's built a whole business on the concept of the self-determined man, his words struck me differently that morning. I lifted up that square of text and re-read it:

> I believe life is constantly testing us for our level of commitment, and life's greatest rewards are reserved for those who demonstrate a never-ending commitment to act until they achieve. This level of resolve can move mountains, but it must be constant and consistent. As simplistic as this may sound, it is still the common denominator separating those who live their dreams from those who live in regret.[xi]

I think he's right, here. There will be no shortage of trials in our lives, so we must not waver as we act and work out the story that's been written for us.

All characters hit a low point before they reach the climax, and eventually, the end. We too must continue living forward through all the ruts and potholes. The faith that there's someone considerably greater than we are, who is deeply contented to help us navigate through obstacles and setbacks to reach our good ending – eternity with Him – gives you and me the steadiness to do so.

———

"Just do it." Really?

That's all this chapter comes down to? You might feel like this all sounds great, but what does it actually mean, practically speaking, to go about "just doing it?"

Well, I think the Nike slogan's beauty is in its simplicity – just like faith. There's not really any formula or complex set of rules to be variably applied to your life based on circumstances.

However, if I were to point out a more tangible and specific takeaway here, it would be that stepping out during frustrating, uncertain, or difficult times becomes manageable when you're following a specific calling. Every character has a unique role to play in a story. This is our "calling." Some might define their calling as working toward a career accomplishment, athletic personal best, or something like financial freedom. I'd argue, however, that these are life goals, and goals are not the same as a calling. A calling is transcendent. It guides the entirety of your life, not just a season or a short-term objective.

Now of course, having a calling also demands that you have a caller. Just like playing a role in a story demands you have an author. A caller or an author must, by definition, be someone outside of and above you – a true calling can't be self-created. When we respond to God, the Great Caller, we'll find a purpose that's far more meaningful than anything we could fabricate ourselves.

This idea of a calling requiring a caller may sound too limiting or too oppressive for some people. Still, in my life, I've found that trusting I have a calling, a Caller, and a Creator has actually made my world so much bigger. I'm not forced to believe the world is confined to the bounds of my pursuits and the limits of my imagination. The borders of my mind are stifling. Because I have a supreme Creator, I'm actually freed to observe all He's made.

Besides, it's just exhausting to play God all the time.

Os Guinness, the author of *The Call*, illustrates this by writing:

> We will never rise higher than when we follow the call not knowing where the path may lead—so long as the Caller is God. And while we may lose our jobs and our health, or retire from a career, we will never retire from our calling—until that Final Call, which is death, leads each of us to the climax and consummation of all calling.... until our life's last day, the passion of our lives is to go further, higher, deeper, always closer to the One who called us once and calls us still–to Himself, and to all the joys knowing him can mean.[xii]

Os says that stepping out is "not only being who we are, but becoming what we are to be," as defined by our Caller. So, if there's to be one practical takeaway here, do you believe you have a calling? If so, do you know what it is, and who's given it to you?

The Chair & the 5th Grader

January 2016

- you only earn grace when you stop trying to -

The backward thing about grace is that in the moment you think you deserve it, or think you need to do something to earn it, you're actually fighting it.

While talks of merging our team into the Washington D.C.-based company progressed, Erin introduced me to a few new people who would become part of my life forever (more accurately, they began to accept me into their lives). My future mother, brother, and sister-in-law all welcomed me with open arms on the first night I met them. We went out for barbecue and ice cream, which I appreciated. I also appreciated that meeting my future in-laws helped me understand Erin with greater depth.

Erin met my family around the same time. She spent a weekend at our family farm while my dad and I hunted, and we went skiing in Colorado with my siblings over New Year's. Erin was the first girl I ever introduced to my family, so after bringing her all the way to Colorado, everyone knew I was serious. They noticed that Erin was serious, too. On the first night my parents met her, my dad whispered to my mom, "I hope Nate realizes this girl is all in."

It was true. She was all in. And I was getting there too. But first, there were a few outstanding and critically important lessons for me to learn. Namely, before I could hit one of my life's highest points – asking Erin to marry me – I needed to internalize how fundamental both giving and accepting grace is to healthy relationships.

You see, every character in every story is deeply flawed. Those flaws keep us fixed on the screen until the movie ends. They glue us to the book until the back cover. Flaws create conflict and conflict requires resolution. We can't help but watch or read until the finale. And while a small sense of resolution may come through an intense car chase or fight scene, watching a broken relationship made whole is what really leaves us satisfied.

Let's say a police officer is taken hostage, but he makes it through a gripping standoff that ends with his partner shooting the criminal. We're not actually excited by the criminal's death. We're excited that because the criminal dies, the officer returns home to see his daughter who perhaps hadn't yet forgiven him for being absent from her childhood. After the officer kisses his wife and his daughter forgives him, we feel a sense of closure. It's their embrace that leaves us raving about the movie. We don't tell go around telling our friends about how many bullet holes were left in the criminal's chest.

You and I are flawed, too. We're not perfect characters. In fact, we'll never meet a perfect person. So, without grace, people would just enter and then forever leave our lives. Grace keeps us connected to each other. It keeps our stories alive, and it keeps them interesting.

———

"See that chair? I'm like that chair. Good for nothing. It just sits there, adding zero value to the world," Daniel said.

I laughed because his statement was ridiculous. It was an amusing analogy, but completely false. Nothing was further from the truth. I sat silent for a moment, studying his expression. I was trying to figure out if he was serious.

"C'mon man," I finally said to him. "We both know that's not true. Where's this coming from?"

"It's always been there; it's just part of me. I have nothing to offer people but they keep me around because I make them feel good about themselves. They're up here," Daniel said, putting his left hand above his head, "and I'm down here." He dropped his right hand below the table.

"What if I like that chair?" I asked.

We were sitting in the bar next door to my apartment. I didn't see anyone within earshot of us. It was quiet for a Friday night but after a long week of work and travel, I was more than content to be somewhere quiet.

I played out Daniel's analogy, "That chair's squeaks are unique. It's well-made, and I like that chair because it's not those other chairs. None of the chairs in here are like *that* chair."

It wasn't working.

"Fine," Daniel said, changing things up on me. "I'm like a fifth grader who's just learning how to dribble and shoot a free throw while you're the NBA player."

I chuckled again, seeing we were headed for nothing more than a downward spiral of analogies.

"Cut me loose! I'm not helping you get better practicing together. Just pull the ripcord man!"

"Daniel, I'm not going to do that. You know that," I said firmly.

Daniel wanted to walk out of my life forever, and it concerned me. I swished my beer and dipped a French fry in it, not realizing that people don't dip fries in beer for good reason. It's gross and clearly why ketchup was invented. My mind was preoccupied, though. Daniel was my best friend. He was trying to push me away because he genuinely thought it was in my best interest.

Now, there's no doubt that if you're the fifth grader learning to shoot hoops, it would be hard to imagine why the NBA player would hang around with you. The idea that Michael Jordan would be delighted to share his time with a little leaguer who completely misses the rim on each shot is hard to accept. But, could Mr. Jordan be there without any expectation that the fifth grader becomes an NBA player? Sure. Maybe he's not there to gain anything. He might enjoy just hanging out in the park. What's wrong with that?

Now, to be clear, I was not the NBA player in this analogy. Daniel was altogether overblowing the fifth grader comparison. I knew I wasn't going to win the argument, however.

"How about I drive you home?" I asked, trying to grab the bill from our waitress before he could.

"Nope, that's what Uber's are for." He shoved his credit card into the black folder and threw my card back at me.

We left the bar and I walked a few doors down to my loft, swiped my key fob on the door, and trotted up to the third floor. "Grace," I said, pausing in the stairwell. That's what Daniel and I were really talking about. Grace can be given to others, but it's something you have to accept for yourself. Grace goes both ways in relationships. I knew I wasn't always gracious with myself, but I was worried about Daniel.

———

The backward thing about grace is that in the moment you think you deserve it, or think you need to do something to earn it, you're actually fighting it. Grace means we're loved for just being ourselves, not for what we have to offer, prove, or what we've accomplished. It's a hard truth to wrap your head around – you find grace when you stop trying to earn it.

> I'd have to trust that my flaws were the ways through which I would receive grace. We don't think of our flaws as the glue that binds us to the people we love, but they are. Grace only sticks to our imperfections. Those who can't accept their imperfections can't accept grace either.[xiii]

"Ah! That's it." I turned off my Kindle and set it down. I was reading Donald Miller's *Scary Close,* and his words so perfectly articulated what I had been trying to communicate to Daniel. I didn't want to lose those words. I feared that if I read anything more, I wouldn't remember to share them with Daniel.

I thought about texting them to Daniel, but was I so perfect that I didn't need to apply them to my own life, first? I started to wonder if I was actually part of the problem.

I had known Daniel longer than anyone, and consciously or subconsciously, I figured I had become a natural measuring stick. I was his point of comparison. If I was always projecting myself to be the NBA player, showing off in an attempt to mask my own fears and shortcomings, that would make really great people feel like fifth graders as a result.

"That's terrible!" I realized suddenly.

One thing was true, though. It had always been much easier for me to give grace than to ask for it. Which makes sense. If you're the one giving grace, you're the NBA player of the relationship. You get to be on the high side of things. Receiving grace, however, makes you vulnerable. It means accepting we're not perfect people.

It's hard to believe that relationships don't grow from perfection; that our flaws and mistakes are the grooves that bind us together. Frankly, it just seems backward. So, once again, we find life is filled with paradox. The very thing we need most to make relationships work – grace – also happens to be the very thing we can never earn or enact by our own power alone.

Feeling slightly overwhelmed, I Googled "grace" to see what I could read. I came across something written by Dr. Trueblood. I had never heard the name before, but something caught my eye as I scanned one of his articles: "We have not advanced very far in our Christian walk unless we have embraced the paradox of freedom; that until we are bound to the Gospel [a message of grace], we are not truly free in ourselves..."[xiv]

The Gospel story tells us that everyone needs grace. It recounts how, starting with that infamous character Adam, we all fall short of God's perfect standard. As a result, we're unable to earn eternal life. Therefore, we depend on grace (why would we even need a God if we were perfect or could gain eternal life through our own actions?).

Dr. Trueblood connects our ability to grow as a person to our recognition that we're screwed up, and that we need some help from outside ourselves. We all need a creator, an author, who can forgive and redeem us.

You can associate Dr. Trueblood's and Mr. Miller's insights in a sort of continual loop. Realizing we need help delivers us from the oppression of perfection. We're then free to accept the Gospel's premise that God accepts us despite our imperfections. This enables us to enter into deeper relationships by sharing the grace we've been given with others. Giving and accepting grace deepens those relationships and in turn, it brings us into greater relational maturity. Greater maturity increases our awareness that we're not perfect, and we do need to give and receive grace (and repeat).

———

Let me rewind my story to years earlier, to a time when I was living in a four-bedroom house with a group of friends. Living in a house of people that aren't family members is like a crash-course on how to give and receive grace. Looking back, it's clear I was in desperate need of that course but at the time, I didn't even realize it was an area in which I was failing. Being gracious was a major blind spot, and it was affecting my relationships.

"Hey man, can we talk?" one of my roommates, Ryan, said as he walked into my room. He turned his shoulders away as he walked in, like he was ready to head right back out if I said no.

"Sure, what's up man?" I inquired as he eased the door shut.

Ryan is one of the most human people I know. I realize that describing someone as "human" may not seem to communicate much, but Ryan never makes himself appear bigger than he is. He's real. He makes you feel comfortable being yourself. He can disarm you by busting into laughter at one of his own jokes. I like that about him. His "shoulder laugh" – you know, the kind where your body shakes and your shoulders bounce as your eyes squint together – makes you forget your reservations. That, combined with an unwavering character and work ethic, makes him perfect for a career managing rich people's money in Dallas, Texas. He's just the kind of true person that people into big-living need.

"I want to tell you some stuff because I love you. I care about you. And I think you should know," Ryan started.

Right away my starship's defense shields went up. Before hearing him out, I told myself this was just Ryan being too sensitive, but I should act attentive for fear of offending him. I figured he was just going to list some things I said and he took too personally.

"Okay, thanks? So, what do I need to know?"

I could feel my mind beginning to drift to other subjects, as if the string of random thoughts inside my head was more interesting than what a good friend had clearly worked up a great deal of courage to say. I was sitting on the edge of my bunk bed and I wondered if Greg, who slept above me, had already heard what Ryan was about to lay out.

"You're a bastard," is what Ryan should have told me. It would have summed everything up perfectly. Ryan's much more gracious than that, however.

"You have this way of making people feel like they're walking on eggshells. People get nervous around you, man. They're scared of what you'll think, what you'll say. You just carry yourself with this hard edge like your way of seeing or doing things is the only way. You don't speak very softly. Personally, it's hurtful."

Ryan listed a few examples of times I had acted insensitively and really hurt him. He demonstrated a pattern that helped me understand this wasn't an isolated incident. He painted a vivid picture of the all-too-real fact that I generally brought a fear-inducing presence into my interactions. He was right, too.

Those who know me today won't believe this as they read it. For a season of my life, however, I was beyond opinionated. I was ruthless. I used my words like daggers. Ryan was totally justified in calling me out but at the time, I shut out his words. Instead of listening, I rationalized the situation as Ryan being overly dramatic. I needed more time to process what he was saying, and I didn't want to say something insensitive given that I was just then coming to grips with my aptitude to do exactly that.

"Do the other guys feel the same way?" I asked, trying to move the conversation toward a close.

"Yeah man, they do. Pretty much everyone does," Ryan said. He stood up, turned toward the door, and said, "Thanks for hearing me out. I care about you, Nate."

Luckily, I was leaving the next day for a weeklong snowboarding trip in Lake Tahoe. Time in the outdoors gave me the chance to move from rejecting Ryan's words to accepting them. It took me the full week to do so, but at the end of my trip, I realized there was a deep cancer rooted inside of me – pride.

My words, interactions, and demeanor were steeped in arrogance. I was hurting the relationships that were supposed to be the most meaningful to me. Thankfully, while I was hurting the people I cared most about, they were also the ones closest enough to notice. Erin hadn't yet entered my life at this point, so I needed Ryan to care enough to call me out.

I discovered the hard way that pride is the complete flipside of grace. It's the anti-grace. If grace binds people together, pride tears people down in a damaging, hurtful way. What's worse is that pride is blinding. It fools you into thinking you don't need grace. When you feel you've reached the heights of perfection, it's easy to feel you're now in charge of determining who does and doesn't receive grace. Pride puts you in the judge's high seat and when you're the one doling out the verdicts, you don't need to be convicted of anything. Yet without conviction, there will never be change.

Ryan lovingly ripped me from my judge's high seat that day. He stopped me from looking down on others in my own little pretend courtroom. I needed Ryan because the more that pride latched onto me, wrapping itself around my heart and mind, the more sightless to its presence in my life I became.

C.S. Lewis calls pride the 'Great Sin' in *Mere Christianity:*

> [T]he more we have it ourselves, the more we dislike it in others... We say that people are proud of being rich, or clever, or good-looking, but they are not. They are proud of being richer, or cleverer, or better looking than others. If everyone else became equally rich, or clever, or good-looking there would be nothing to be proud about.[xv]

Lewis says that pride is competitive by nature. It forces us into conflict with each other. If we're concerned with who's better looking or higher achieving, or we're focused on pointing out someone else's flaws in an attempt to elevate ourselves, when will we ever find the time to ask for grace in the areas we need it most?

Through a combination of time, Ryan's words, Lewis' writing, and God's grace, I realized that when I pointed out someone else's flaws, I was actually calling out the mistakes and weaknesses I disliked within myself. If I needed to feel accomplished or talented, the easiest way to achieve that was to ensure the people around me were losers, right?

————

So, back to that squeaky bar chair and the fifth grader. I was only able to point out the talent and worth I saw in Daniel because years before, I stopped trying to one-up the guy next to me. Thanks to Ryan handing me a shovel, I had done the hard work of uprooting the pride controlling my life. I was a work-in-progress, but I was ready to talk about grace in Daniel's life.

Over a period of weeks and months, Daniel and I sustained our conversation about grace. As he dug his heels in, I shared about the areas of life for which I needed grace. The turning point in our conversations came (no kidding) after Daniel was at a Jeep dealer and saw a tricked-out Wrangler. He bought it without hesitation and the flood gates opened.

After rolling off the lot in that new Jeep, Daniel began what is perhaps the healthiest season of growth I've ever witnessed in a friend. He discovered that he loved off-roading, camping, wake surfing, the outdoors, and being an all-around solid friend. He found a girlfriend who enjoys being with him, too. Those interests returned his God-given energy and vitality. He liked who he was becoming, and he learned to give himself a little more grace. Daniel had always been a life-giving presence to me, so it was good to see him thrive again.

Which side of grace do you typically fall on? If you prefer to be the one who gives grace, is it possible you need to ask for grace, too? If you've been hesitant to extend grace to someone who's asked, do you need to reach out to them this week?

I Think I Need a Break (Part 1)

May – June 2016

- it's easiest to hurt those you love most -

I knew her worst fear was that I'd leave and walk out on her.
What I didn't know, before that moment, was how easy it is to hurt
those you love most. When you lash out, the people closest to you
will be the first to bear the scars.

———————

C hange is an integral part to any gripping story. We grow bored and disinterested without change, whether it's one character growing from snooty and snobby to lovable and adorable, or new characters being introduced and shifting the dynamic. Change is a constant in any engaging story, and it always follows an "arc" – a steady trajectory that guides the tone and pace of the storyline.

Within that prevailing arc, the protagonist – the main character – needs to encounter an antagonist – the villain who works against him or her. But in some cases, the protagonist simply slides backward during some type of internal struggle.

I think this type of internal struggle aligns with our own experiences. Our nastiest and most ensnaring battles often rise up from within us. Battles like depression, selfishness, and anger are the worst because they feel like friendly fire. They're confusing, disheartening, and they don't offer any outside enemies to fight back against.

At this point of the story, my internal conflicts began to spill over and affect those around me. Namely, Erin. My struggle to apply what I had been learning in previous chapters – work, rest, staying present – began to affect our growing relationship. As we grew closer, our company began to merge and transition our staff into the Washington D.C. office. My life grew crowded, and my thinning margin started to impact Erin directly.

———

"I think I just need a break," I remarked, looking at Erin as I sat on my kitchen island.

Erin looked away, concerned. She said very softly, "Oh..." before her words trailed off.

I wasn't expecting that reaction. By "I need a break," I meant I felt trapped. I wanted to express that life wasn't giving me enough room to breathe. Each day and week had become increasingly structured. My schedule was filled with all very good things, like double-dates with friends, family dinners, birthday parties, travel, and work, but that type of schedule was suffocating me. I was trying to communicate that I needed more breathing room amidst all the pre-planned activity.

Erin and I had been dating for six months at this point. I was still adjusting to the idea of sharing my time with someone else. Dividing my time meant compromising on the ambitions to which I still stubbornly clung. Compared to my friends, I've always been the most independent, so this was difficult for me. I relish three-hour bike rides alone and going out to eat at a table for one. Most of my friends would rather peel corn husks while wearing oven mitts.

On this particular night, my friends Nate and Sarah came over to my loft for dinner. I grilled fish and steak tacos and we shared some amazing conversation. Nate and Sarah were pregnant with twins, and it had been months since I last saw them. By all counts, it was a night well-spent and I had chosen to put it on our calendar. It was also, however, the last night of a long week that left me feeling like a caged bird.

You've had those weeks before, right?

I grew quiet after Nate and Sarah left. Too quiet. I retreated into my shell as Erin and I started to wash dishes. Some people become grouchy or testy when they're frustrated. I simply shut down. Erin noticed, and she asked me what was wrong.

"Nothing," I said in a tone suggesting the exact opposite. I wanted to dismiss the conversation.

Erin pressed me, "You're not saying anything. Something's not okay when you get quiet."

"I'm just tired," I said, hopping up onto the kitchen island and continuing to sidestep the conversation.

"Nate, you can talk to me – of all people. You know that, right?"

I looked at the ground. I thought about my options before finally asking her, "Do you ever feel like the fire inside you is dying? Like, that little flame is being put out?"

Erin hesitated. "No, not really. What are you saying, exactly?"

"I don't know. Just that I guess."

My brain has this funny way of insulating itself from distressing conversations when I'm worn thin. It shuts down and I have to work really hard to reengage in the discussion. I'll never win any awards for my ability to verbally articulate the emotions swirling inside me, but asking me to do so when I'm tired is like asking a walrus to climb a tree. It just won't end well.

So, of course, that's what happened next.

"Nate, what are you trying to say?" Erin pressed, her voice thick with concern.

I knew I had to answer, I couldn't just sit in silence. Erin would grow too anxious. "I think I just need a break," I finally said, looking down at Erin from the kitchen island.

She looked away, disturbed. She began to speak but fell silent.

———

Erin's worst fear is that I'll walk out on her without warning. My "I need a break" comment sounded like the start of leaving her, so she couldn't continue the conversation. She began to shut down as well. It was a gut-level reaction for her, not a choice. I'd awoken a deep fear lying dormant within her. My words had located and released an ocean of insecurity that washed over her.

She walked away from me, falling into distress. She didn't look sad. She just looked panicked. There were no tears at first; she was too overwhelmed to cry. As I remained on the kitchen island and Erin backed away, the physical distance growing between us personified something very frightening to me. I realized that my words, unchecked and self-centered, had just hurt someone I loved very much.

I jumped down from the island and followed her to the living room couch. She curled up inside the corner of the sectional's curve and began to sob deep, involuntary tears. She looked up to the ceiling, struggling to keep her tears from brimming over. They welled up and spilled down her cheeks anyway.

I sank into the couch and tried to wrap her in a hug to say I was sorry. I needed her to understand I'd only miscommunicated. I hadn't meant what she thought I meant. But to no one's surprise, she didn't want my hug. And why would she? In that moment, she thought she had to return to living life on her own. It wasn't that she was scared of independence; she was scared of losing someone she loved. Worse, she feared she was losing me because she'd killed the "fire" inside me. While I was only trying to make things better, I made an already bad situation worse. She pushed back against my hug and began to hyperventilate. Her chest heaved with uncontrollable sobs.

Did you know it's easiest to hurt those you love most? When you lash out, the people closest to you are the first to bear the scars. I didn't want to hurt Erin. I wasn't trying to, but I had done so nonetheless. I had no clue what to do next.

I thought to myself, "Do I say something? No, that didn't work out so well last time. That's why we're here in the first place. Should I give her another hug? No, she didn't like that. Maybe I should just wait. What else can I do?"

I sat next to her, lost. I decided it was all I could do in the moment. Shortly after my internal debate, Erin regained control of her breathing. The fear of not being able to breathe had overpowered the fear of me walking out on her. She told herself to breathe, calming herself enough that I was able to draw closer and whisper to her.

"Erin, I'm sorry. I'm really sorry. I don't want to leave you, but what I communicated sounded like that. What I said was scary, and I'm sorry."

I left it there. I didn't want to complicate things by trying to translate what I originally intended. It didn't matter anymore. At that point, I was feeling something different. Mostly, I was afraid that I had permanently damaged her trust in me.

"You just scared me. I'm okay. I just feel startled," she eventually whispered. I took that as my queue to hold her.

"I just don't want to lose you. My heart can't handle that again," Erin explained.

Erin had lost her father, Mike, to cancer four years prior. From every story I've heard about Mike, he was a joyful man full of life and a contagious personality. He always wanted to be with people, especially his family. Erin will forever know how much he loved her. Even though he told her so every day, he never needed to say it. Erin could just tell. Every fiber of his being and every breath of his life let her know how much he cared for her.

I often wish I had the chance to meet him. While I would have enjoyed his favorite, extra-sausage pizza, more importantly, I would have seen Erin smile in a way that only her dad can make her smile. Erin loved him very much and as she began to love me, she feared she'd eventually lose me, too. While she had pushed past that fear for months, I reignited it with a few careless words, "I need a break."

Erin's love had given me the spade to unearth her greatest joys, but also her greatest anxieties.

We sat in the corner of my sectional for another hour, watching the rain fall on the cars zooming down North Avenue. As we sat, I considered my newfound and very alarming paradox; it's easiest to hurt those you love most. Erin processed a discovery of her own as we sat listening to the rain. Our love was the source of so much peace and joy in her life, but it was also the gateway to her greatest fears.

I Think I Need a Break (Part 2)

July 2016

- it's easiest to hurt those you love most -

There are no ordinary people. You have never talked to a mere mortal. Nations, cultures, arts, civilizations – these are mortal, and their life is to ours as the life of a gnat. But it is immortals whom we joke with, work with, marry, snub and exploit – immortal horrors or everlasting splendors.

———————

E rin and I survived that night okay. While life didn't slow down as much as I'd hoped, I learned the power of my words, and how they can either build others up or tear others down. However, I hadn't yet learned that the absence of words can damage a treasured relationship in the same way that the wrong words can.

This time, I hurt my sister, Rachael. Not intentionally, I never meant to upset her. Just as I hadn't expected to hurt Erin with those stupid words, "I need a break."

Initially, I didn't even notice that I had hurt Rachael. As Erin and I spent more time together, building a strong foundation for what would eventually turn into our marriage, I was trying to balance too much. I was traveling four to five days each week as we began the process of merging companies. I was transitioning out of a small group and leadership role at our church, and I was trying to keep ties with all of my existing friendships while meeting and getting to know Erin's friends, too.

At the same time, there was still a selfish part of me that hadn't died off. I was craving my old single, independent interests. I wanted to prioritize things like long bike rides alone, backpacking trips, and building things out of wood. You know, the stuff that makes guys feel good about themselves.

My relationship with Rachael had always been the strongest in my world. We grew up 18 months apart and matched each other's driven, stubborn personalities. We were worst enemies and best friends throughout childhood. As we moved away from our family's home for college, we managed to deepen that bond. Rachael transferred from Tennessee to the University of Illinois, where I was, after her freshman year. I was elated when I learned she was transferring and those years cemented our friendship. She always knew what I was thinking when we were together.

I was counting on Rachael to continue her uncomplicated and straight-forward approach to living as the free time in my life decreased. I carried on dating, traveling, and doing all the good things that filled each day, assuming that our relationship would be as it always had been. I figured Rachael was living her life – she was planning her own wedding just six weeks away and pursuing a career in medicine – and I was living mine. I thought we'd just pick up where we left off when we were together again.

I knew I wanted to marry Erin at this point. Given all the major life decisions I was facing, I also knew I wanted to marry her soon. It was important that Erin and I started making important choices together, like what city I'd be living in. Because Rachael was getting married at the end of July, I decided to propose at the end of August. That meant I'd begin talking with my family shortly before Rachael's wedding.

I have three siblings; Rachael, Rebekah, and Phil. Phil has our family's artistic genes. He's creative and he's curious. He likes to figure out how to rebuild, improve, and design things. He'd build his own skateboards in our basement or turn videos of his everyday life into captivating short films, just because he was bored and wanted to learn something new. We say Phil will be the most successful out of us four. He's that naturally gifted. He's also the most laid back, so I knew he was just happy I found someone I loved.

Figuring that I already knew Rachael's and Phil's thoughts on me marrying Erin, I decided to see what Rebekah thought first.

Rebekah has an amazing ability to know what others are

feeling, as if they had written it across their foreheads. She's always been my sensitive sister, especially when compared to Rachael's straight-talk. Her emotional intelligence had skyrocketed in the previous two years after she moved to Grand Rapids. It was like the distance only sharpened her sense for our family's dynamic. I really valued her opinion, too. Rebekah knew me, she knew Erin, and she would be able to process our conversation emotionally – in addition to hearing the words I was speaking.

I decided to call her as I jogged through the National Mall in D.C. I stopped near the retaining wall surrounding the Washington Monument and opened FaceTime.

"Hey girlie, what's happening?"

We talked about life in Grand Rapids and caught up on her own relationship before I asked, "I want to marry Erin, and I want your input. What do you think about us?"

After asking me some thoughtful questions about why I wanted to marry Erin, Rebekah gave me her blessing with one caveat, "I love Erin, and I love you with her, too – that's important. But I think you need to talk to Rachael next."

"I plan to, but tell me what you mean by that," I inquired.

"Well, she feels out of the loop, and it's hurting her. You're moving to D.C., you're getting married, and your life's changing at the same time her life is. It's all happening very quickly."

We talked for a while longer and I thanked her before running back to my Airbnb. I was as impressed with Rebekah's ability to loop me into what I had missed, as I was confused by how I'd evidently upset Rachael.

I thought that sharp words, not a lack of them, hurt people.

I texted Rachael as I walked into my Airbnb, "Hey girlie, what are you up to Thursday? Dinner?" She texted me back a few hours later, agreeing and saying she wanted sushi.

———

"Southwest Flight 2521 has been cancelled. You may rebook your ticket for an alternate, equal fare or request your funds be returned to your method of payment."

I looked at the email on my phone in disbelief. It was Thursday, the day I was planning to meet Rachael. I was about to miss the dinner I had arranged precisely because she felt I was missing from her life. I texted her that I was working on getting home, but I wasn't sure what time I'd be able to make our dinner.

I sat down in Washington Reagan National Airport and opened up my computer to see if there were other flights, other airlines, or any other way to get a flight into Chicago. United had a flight leaving around the same time for a few hundred dollars extra. I booked it without hesitation and scrambled to get to the next terminal in time. One flight, a pack of peanuts, and a brisk walk through Midway brought me to a cab waiting to sweep me out of the city for sushi in the suburbs.

It was raining and gray, which I thought somewhat appropriately mirrored my current mood. The rain's intensity increased as my driver turned onto the highway. The downpour was strong enough that I couldn't hear the keystrokes on my laptop. I had left for the airport earlier than I normally would, so I was on the hook to create some last-minute reports for the team back in D.C. However, the more I typed, the more frustrated I became. It occurred to me that the very reason I was going to have dinner with Rachael was the same reason I had my laptop open in the backseat.

Time. I didn't have a lot of it, and I hadn't spent it very well during the last few months. I was always on-the-go from one place to another. I closed my laptop and leaned back in my seat. I looked through the sunroof and thought about what I had done – or hadn't done – to drive a wedge into a treasured relationship.

People tell me I'm smart and engaging and as a result, I've always had lots of opportunity. Business, church, volunteer groups, friends, hobbies; they've all offered me a full life. As I took on more activities, they all competed for my time and attention. I'm no exception here, by the way. It's the same for you and in everyone's world. The more you live, the more you develop, and the more opportunities you're given.

The difference is that I skew toward a more driven, self-motivated extreme than most people. So, while believing I could handle it all, I attempted to take on whatever commitments were offered to me. It was – and still is – tempting to accept promotions, leadership roles, and a multitude of other activities while believing I'm competent enough to do it all (and do it well).

What I hadn't yet realized, however, is that the more I say "yes" to opportunities, the more I need to say "no" to maintain balance. I'm a limited person; I'm not infinite. As my influence and calling rose, I needed to become commensurately more judicious with where and how I invested my time. When I didn't do that, I dramatically reduced my ability to intentionally invest in the people I loved.

That investment is important because over the long run, people aren't static. Relationships, therefore, aren't static either. They're living, dynamic, and ever-shifting. Rachael knew this. She felt that during a time of rapid change for her – marriage, medical school, etc. – our historically consistent relationship was also changing.

I had unconsciously dipped into a relationship that never wavered, in order to afford extra time for other areas of my life. Rachael and I had always maintained a solid relationship, so I didn't check my strategy until it was too late. She noticed weeks had passed since I last called simply to say, "I love you, and I'm thinking about you." I shut my laptop and tuned into the thoughts running through my mind. I considered how often I blurred the line between spoken word and internal thought. What's between my ears doesn't always make it to my lips.

"It's so simple," I muttered. It occurred to me that meaningful interactions don't always have to be big performances. Grand gestures don't build relationships. Quiet consistency and simple notes that say, "I'm thinking about you," are all it takes.

Factoring in city traffic, the driver's GPS said we'd have another 35 minutes in the car before arriving at the restaurant. I sat back and meditated on what Erin had told me over dinner one week prior. Erin reminded me that we should spend the greatest amount of time together because we're the most important relationship we have. She talked about how more established relationships shouldn't be short-changed when I want to invest time into another area of my life.

Although Erin used different words to communicate it, she clued me in to part two of the same paradox – it's easiest to hurt those you love most. She was teaching me to spend my time, energy, and thoughtful words on the people closest to me. Erin was, once again, a step ahead in regard to what I needed to learn.

As my driver carried on through the deluge, I thought about the masterful design behind it all. As God wrote and planned out His story of the world, He didn't create us to do it all. That's not our part to play. He created sleep and hunger to remind us of that. God even gave us an example through Jesus' life. Jesus –

whether you believe in his divinity or not – was, without a doubt, one of history's greatest influencers. Yet Jesus invested his time in traveling with and relating to a group of just 12 people. As his ministry grew, churches, cities, and literal mobs of people all wanted more of his attention. Still, Jesus consistently focused his teaching and time on only 12 disciples.

———

The host led me to a booth near the back of the restaurant. I slid in facing the blank wall instead of the hubbub of people and waiters rushing around. I wanted to focus on Rachael's words without being distracted.

"Why are you smiling?" Rachael asked as she slid into her side of the booth.

I couldn't help but smile. "Oh, I just like this. Normally we'd be in the middle of a long run talking like this. Talking over food is just as good though."

"It just all feels really fast," Rachael got right to it. "A move and a marriage are big things, you know."

"Yeah, and I agree, but I think they're made faster by the fact that I haven't looped you into the progress we've made over time. That's my fault," I explained. "But I also think that with both of our lives growing quickly, and in different directions, it feels twice as fast."

"Okay, I guess. I know this works both ways, too. I guess I just miss it," she said, referring to the days when we'd go for a long run just to be together.

"Me too."

After a brief pause I offered, "I do think it's pretty cool we'll be moving through the same stage of life together. You know? New in-laws and that kind of stuff at the same time."

"But in two different cities," Rachel pointed out.

"True, but we never thought I'd stay in Chicago. Besides, remember when you were in Tennessee? We visited each other a few times. We probably grew closer during that year than in any other."

"Yeah, yeah." Rachael rolled her eyes with a cheeky grin.

I grabbed a piece of her sushi with my chopsticks. As she did the same, I thought about how her friendship had molded my personality. I certainly owed the resolve and stubborn fight within me to her. I supposed who I spent my time with wasn't just about the people I was called to invest in. It was equally about the people who had been called to shape me.

"You know I'm excited for you, right?" Rachael offered, studying my response.

"Yeah, I know. And I want to tell you how excited I am for you more often," I replied while snatching the bill from our server.

———

Rachael walked me to a nearby train station so I could catch a ride back into the city. Once I was on the train's bench seats with my bright green duffel bag preventing anyone from sitting near me, I slipped a thin book by CS Lewis, *Weight of Glory*, out of my bag. I flipped through the pages until I came to an underlined paragraph I had read earlier that week:

> *There are no ordinary people. You have never talked to a mere mortal. Nations, cultures, arts, civilizations – these are mortal, and their life is to ours as the life of a gnat. But it is immortals whom we joke with, work with, marry, snub and exploit – immortal horrors or everlasting splendors.*[xvi]

Here, Mr. Lewis shows us that our relationships are infinitely more important than any type of leadership position, degree, accomplishment, corporate title, or momentary fame. People are immortal, yet so often we choose to invest our time in what will one day fade away.

On the flipside, our words, if we choose to use them intentionally and consistently, can be one of the most enduring legacies we leave. Our words enrich and shape the stories of those we care about most. And, who knows? Your words might even go so far as to lift someone up from a downward spiral, giving them the hope they need to thrive during a frustrating or disappointing season of life.

I think we miss this reality because exchanging short sentences with familiar friends and family members never feels consequential. It's much easier to find meaning in the striking accomplishments and outstanding achievements that don't happen to us every day. Unfortunately, it took my own unforced errors in my relationships with Erin and Rachael to recognize this. Hopefully for you, it only requires reading this chapter.

Bunk Beds and Beaches (Part 1)

August 2016

- your biggest life changes develop the fastest -

"Your single self has to go away; you'll be engaged," Greg said
bluntly. "Life changes don't always build slowly. The biggest
ones happen the fastest. It's backward, I know."

Within a few weeks of eating sushi with Rachael, Erin's older brother, Ryan, was driving me around their childhood neighborhood. As soon as I said I wanted to marry Erin, he wanted me to know more of their family's history. He drove me around their old house, neighborhood park, school, gym, and more. Essentially, Ryan shared the chapters from their lives long before I arrived on the scene. I really appreciated that, maybe more than he knows. We finished the tour with hot dogs, fries, and milkshakes, which I also appreciated.

I actually had the ring I was going to propose with at this point of the story. Erin was unaware, but My grandfather had given me my late grandmother's diamond a few years prior. He'd ask me every once and a while, "So, did you find her yet?" Followed by, "You know I'm not getting any younger, right?" I'd smile and say he wasn't going anywhere, but I was working on finding her.

A few months before the start of this chapter, Erin met me at a jewelry shop to try on rings. Before she arrived, I gave my grandmother's diamond to the jeweler and he tucked it away in his safe. Then, after Erin walked in, he pulled out the diamond as if it was the top stone he recommended for her. She tried it on with different bands and we eventually found a setting she liked. I lingered in the shop until Erin left and then I paid for it.

Erin's mother, Kathy, and I went out to dinner after I met with Ryan and bought the ring. We talked for several hours about more family stories. She has a story for every occasion, and the amount of detail she remembers is incredible. As I left that dinner, I decided I wanted to propose before Labor Day. Erin and I had already planned to spend the week before in Vail with some friends, Greg and Elise. She'd come to love the mountains during our trips over the last year, so it would make the perfect setting.

———

"Why don't you just buy this ring so we can get married tomorrow?" Erin joked as she picked up a $7 silver band from one of those typical airport stores that sells books and luggage. It was Thursday night, and we were standing in Chicago's Midway

Airport waiting to board our flight to Denver.

"Yeah... it'd be pretty crazy if I proposed this weekend, right?" I teased, trying to conceal my complete seriousness.

"You know I don't need a big fancy ring, right?" Erin asked as we walked down the eternal rows of seats in the B terminal.

"I do, but thanks for saying it anyway."

I glanced behind us. Greg was smiling, and Elise was stifling her laughter. Our trip to Vail was actually Greg's suggestion – it was Elise's birthday week and he surprised her with tickets to see The Head and the Heart in concert at Red Rocks Amphitheatre.

The next morning, while Greg and Elise distracted Erin with coffee at a café in Breckenridge, I called a creek-side restaurant to speak with the chef about a special menu. It was the same place my parents dined at as newlyweds. Greg and I had planned out the next day so that after he and Elise left for their concert, Erin and I would hike Vail Mountain. Once I found an overlook that felt breathtaking enough to serve as our backdrop, I'd propose, and we'd celebrate with a special dinner after.

Back at our condo that night, Greg and I laid in our bunk beds chatting. It was almost poetic that we were sleeping in bunks. From planning out our lives during our college years, to talking about what marriage would be like as we traveled in the years following, we always seemed to exchange our most memorable conversations with Greg leaning over a bunk's top railing.

I didn't feel nervous, but I didn't feel overly excited, either. I guess I didn't know how I was supposed to feel. "How do you feel something when you're not there yet?" I mused.

"I don't know man. I guess it's good to just feel what you feel sometimes. You shouldn't have to feel anything particular – that's never really been your style anyways. You're pretty even-keeled." Greg reminded me.

"That is true," I agreed.

"Alright man, I'm gonna read and then go to sleep. You should do the same. Big day and all." Greg rolled over for the night.

"Good idea." I thought about the emotions I should have been feeling as I tried to fall sleep. I finally decided it was okay to not feel anything in particular as I drifted off.

———

My watch said 4:15 a.m. but I was wide awake. At first, I laid still, futilely hoping I'd fall back asleep if I gave myself enough time. When that didn't work, I decided it was alright to lay awake and think for a few hours. It was a decisive day, after all. Erin and I would officially begin "our" story that afternoon.

I was still feeling relatively neutral about the day when an alarming thought elbowed its way into my mind. The thought told me there was still time; Erin didn't know I was going to propose. If I wanted to, I could just keep the ring and not propose.

I could take more time – I didn't need to commit to anything.

Do you remember what we said about conflict in the earlier chapters? That a story's conflict is sometimes rooted in an outside antagonist, but other times, it's an internal struggle? This moment was a bit of both. It very much felt like a direct and outside influence was trying to sway me, but it targeted my inner insecurities. It taunted me. While I was wholly committed to marrying Erin, I couldn't shake the idea that I still had a choice. What if living life uncommitted was the better choice?

I knew that I wouldn't, but I *could* decide not to propose.

"Greg man, you up?" After failing to wrestle my emotions into submission, I felt it was okay to wake him up.

"Uh, yeah," Greg whispered. "I'm not sure why, I don't even think the sun's awake."

I laughed, "No, no it's not. But I'm glad you're up."

"Yeah? Why's that?" Greg mumbled.

"I keep having this thought. This is the last hour to live my life and after, I die. I don't mean literally die, of course. But like, once I get down on a knee, there's no turning back. It's permanent, you know? I can't go back. And it's my choice to make. I don't actually have to propose today. As long as I lie here, it's a choice that just sits in front of me."

I continued rambling for a few more minutes. Greg, still

groggy with sleep, did his best to keep up. "I've prepared for this and I know without a doubt I love Erin. I want to marry her, but we're here now. I realize I'm gaining a wife, but I can't help but feel there's a part of me that dies today, and… well… yeah."

I could have sputtered on, letting my thoughts shake Greg awake, but I decided to shut up.

"Well, there is. Your single self has to go away now; you'll be engaged," Greg said bluntly. "Life changes doesn't always build slowly. The biggest ones happen the fastest. It's backward, I know."

"Right! I just feel like it's already my wedding day. Like, as soon as I'm down on one knee, I'm committing to Erin for the rest of my life. So I guess, in a way, this does mean today's my wedding day. I've made my choice after this."

"Yeah man. You're basically getting married in 10 hours. That's a big deal," Greg said as reached into my bunk to put his hand on my shoulder. "I want to pray for you."

Greg prayed in a way I hadn't heard before. While talking to God, he reminded me that our world changed forever on a single day, Good Friday. He talked about how God's son died on a cross to offer us eternal life. In the same way, my formerly single-self had to die so that I could gain a new life – a life with Erin. He said my life wouldn't be the same after today, but God knew how our story would turn out in the end. I couldn't see it now, but in leaving my selfishness behind, I would gain a much more full and joyful life as Erin's husband.

I turned Greg's words around in my head. I considered how I couldn't gain anything (or more precisely, anyone) if I didn't first give up something (my comfortably single life). I thought about how quickly my life's most significant choice had crept up on me, and how glad I was that Greg was lying in the top bunk.

We sat in bed for a few more minutes, not saying much. There wasn't much else to say. There was just a choice to make. By stepping out of bed, I knew I'd be starting the process of proposing so I took another minute to reiterate my commitment to cherish Erin forever. Then I stood up, touched the ring sitting inside my backpack, and walked into the living room.

Erin was sitting on the living room couch sipping coffee from an oversized mug. "Finally!" she sighed. "I've been wondering if you'd ever get out of bed."

"It's not that late," I defended, keeping a few feet of distance between us. I thought she might have been able to smell my secret on me. I wanted to be certain she didn't have a clue I was about to pop the question.

"I heard you guys talking when I went to the bathroom. You talked for a while, you know." She stopped short of asking about our topic of conversation.

"Oh, yeah, we've been awake for a bit I guess. It was good to catch up with Greg," I said before quickly changing the subject. "Hungry?"

"Yes, but you never gave me my kiss. Priorities." Erin smiled, pointing out that I had broken our morning routine. I always kiss Erin before doing anything else in the mornings.

"How could I forget the most important part of breakfast?" I walked to the couch and kissed her before retreating back into the kitchen.

———

I swaddled the ring box inside my rain jacket and tucked it into my backpack. I must have touched my backpack over a hundred times that day, just to ensure the ring was still there. Greg parked our car near the base of Vail Mountain to drop Erin and I off. As I stepped out, Greg grabbed my arm and whispered, "I'm proud of you, Nateman." Elise smiled a little brighter and turned away, suppressing her squeals so that Erin wouldn't hear.

"Thanks, you guys have fun today too. I'll see you on the other side," I kept half of my body in the car to block Erin from hearing the conversation.

"Ready?" I asked Erin, really directing the question at myself.

"Yep!"

I felt settled by the time we hit our trail, Berry Picker. I was back to my trademark even-keeled self. Only 2,200 vertical feet stood between me and the path to marriage. I liked the idea of a challenging hike before proposing. We'd save our breath on the way up and I was, for obvious reasons, more into thinking than talking. Navigating through rocks, aspens, and mountain bikes on the way to the mountaintop felt appropriately symbolic. I wasn't sure what the symbolism was exactly, but if I was about to find my better half in marriage, it seemed fitting to embark on that journey by ascending a mountain.

We passed a slow-moving family one hour into our hike. They were progressing at a glacial pace, catering to a little boy who couldn't decide if he preferred to tolerate the boredom of being carried up in a backpack or endure the exhaustion of climbing up under his own willpower. I figured that if he was half my height, and I'd gain over 2,000 vertical feet, he would effectively have to hike up 4,000 feet.

Shortly thereafter, we crossed paths with a middle-school aged girl sitting on a fallen tree. "Are you with that family back there?" I asked.

"Yeah, those are my parents. And my little brother," she groaned. "They're really slow."

"Is it okay for you to keep hiking?" Erin inquired.

"Yes, it's fine. They know I'm okay. I have a cell phone," she explained, pulling a pink cellphone case from her pocket.

"Alright then, want to hang with us for a bit?" Erin offered.

The girl nodded emphatically. I was also glad to have a new companion. It meant I didn't have to talk as much. That was important because I'm no good at talking and thinking at the same time. I start sentences that trail off midway through them as I continue the conversation in my head. It frustrates some people but Erin just thinks it's funny. She knows that if I'm not speaking, I'm often pondering something. She doesn't always ask what's happening "up there" in the moment, but she usually has a good idea.

We swapped questions with our middle-school travel buddy for another mile before she decided to drop back and wait for her family. I broke out our sandwiches as we continued hiking and within the hour, we were standing at the top.

"Looks like rain," I told Erin, gazing at the foreboding clouds gathering above us.

"Want to eat the rest of lunch in Eagle's Nest?" She pointed to the looming brick structure perched atop Vail Mountain.

"Sounds good to me." I knew our engagement photos would turn out much sharper in the sunlight. We found a bench in Eagle's Nest to wait out the rain. 30 minutes later, I was ready for a nap. My early wake-up, mental gymnastics, and the hike had all caught up to me.

"You want to nap? Now?" Erin probed, "You feeling okay?"

"Yeah, I'm fine. Just tired," I assured her. It was the truth, too.

I was simply worn down. Greg's prayer gave me peace and I was confident I was ready to ask Erin to marry me. I had already transferred the ring to my shorts' zipper pocket, keeping it at the ready. I just felt drained. We laugh about that now. The idea I'd take a nap before proposing cracks Erin up.

I laid down on a wooden bench, closed my eyes, and drifted off for a power nap.

———

"Ready?" Erin asked, seeing that the sun was shining and I was beginning to stir.

"Yep, let's go." I rolled off my bench, tapping the ring in my shorts pocket for good measure.

"Let's hike toward Game Creek Bowl. Near the overlook trail on the rim," I pointed to a southern trail running along a deep valley of aspen and pine trees.

"Sounds good to me," Erin smiled and pulled out her phone. "Picture first!"

As Erin snapped a photo, I rehearsed the plan in my head. We'd trek along Ridge Route and once we arrived at a spot with an attractive-enough overlook, I'd suggest we take another picture. I'd use my backpack to prop up my phone and tell Erin I was setting a self-timer. In reality, I'd start a video and walk back to where she'd be waiting.

I felt relaxed, which I was grateful for. My signature poise hadn't betrayed me. Erin had no idea I was about to ask her the most important question of my life, nor that I held my single most valuable treasure – my grandmother's diamond – zippered inside my waistband.

We came to a bend in the path and the trail exposed a beautiful overlook. We could see for a clear five miles. The mountainside was speckled with blankets of yellow wildflowers and it sloped downward before intersecting the crystal blue sky. Now this was a view Erin would love to look at for years to come.

"Hey, why don't we get a picture here? This is a great spot," I suggested.

"Great idea. How do you want to take it?" she asked.

"I'll set my phone on my backpack with a timer. Can you go into the field, over there? So I know where to aim the camera?"

Erin beamed as she floated among the wildflowers. "Here!" she called, picking her spot.

"Alright, one second!" I set up the video, started it, stopped it, and started it once more. I wasn't taking any chances.

Before walking back down to Erin, I slipped a manila envelope out of my backpack. It had a fancy seal and the letter "E" on the outside. I never had the chance to meet Mike, Erin's father, before he passed, so I decided to write out the words I would have said to him inside a card. I think best while writing, and it was important that I got those words right.

One of my good friends, JJ, got married one month before this. He pulled me aside before I left his wedding and said, "My one regret in asking Bri to marry me is that I didn't write anything down. It didn't come out like I wanted. It's just really hard to remember everything you want to say in that moment. Write it down."

It was good advice. Erin loves letters, too. I write her love notes fairly often so she wasn't suspicious when she saw the envelope. She smiled wide and swayed back and forth with anticipation. She tucked her hands behind her back to prevent her excitement from spilling over.

When she asked why I was holding a letter, I said I wanted to make her smile for the picture. She liked that idea, but when she went to reach for it, I told her I'd read it aloud.

"Oh, I like that even better," she glowed.

She quickly realized this wasn't a letter addressed to her. I was speaking to Mike. Somehow, she still didn't know I was going to propose at this point. She supposed I was being extra thoughtful.

As I finished reading the letter, with fresh tears trickling down her cheeks, Erin swung her arms around me in a giant bear hug. I hugged her with one arm, and with the other, I unzipped my waistband pocket. I fished out the ring and released our embrace. Then, kneeling, I raised the diamond and asked Erin to marry me.

She didn't actually say yes. She just squeaked.

Erin clasped her cheeks in shock, twisting in uncontrolled excitement. Squeals of joy echoed from the peaks. Using her thumbs and forefingers, she plucked the ring from my hands. She slipped it onto her finger and extended her hand to admire the fit. It wasn't exactly how I'd seen it done before. I imagined I'd slowly slide the ring onto her finger as she cried "yes!" It was very "Erin," however. Plus, I captured it all on video.

As we hiked back to Eagle's Nest, Erin called her mom and a few close friends to relay the good news. Soon after, the rain picked up and shut us inside the lodge. As we waited for a pocket of lightning to pass, Erin used the downtime to call more family and friends. I listened, smiling, feeling confident in my choice.

I wasn't sure if our story would be easygoing, stressful, tumultuous, or smooth, but I was certain it would surpass any life I could have lived alone. Although my life's most defining moment had snuck up on me, I recognized that choosing to leave behind the comforts of my formerly single life was the gateway to a far more meaningful story.

———

Looking back to one year before my proposal, a good friend from Texas, Dave, had called me after my first non-date date with Erin. I leaned against my bike outside my loft as we talked, and I lamented that I wasn't so sure I was ready to date. In my mind, there was still too much I wanted to see and achieve. I feared I'd lose my ability to experience all I craved on my own terms if I started dating more seriously.

Dave firmly stated that marriage is *not* about gaining something for yourself. It's about sacrifice. It's about sharing your life with someone. In the process of doing so, you hope to in turn find a joy that's more fulfilling than any selfish pursuit. He asserted that if I wasn't ready to consider spending my life with someone – marrying someone – then I shouldn't be going out on date number two. Of course, I wouldn't know if I wanted to marry Erin unless we went out again, but the principle was that if I, personally, wasn't in a healthy enough place to consider commitment, I had no business dating a woman who was.

I had to confront the same reservations I had before dating when it was time to advance beyond dating. I should have seen it coming. But then again, we're not authors. We're characters, and stories usually contain some type of plot twist right before the climax. As I laid in that bunk bed, anticipating a high point in life, there was no way to know I'd need to snuff out the desire to escape to independence before proposing.

I did know, however, that our now-joined story was about something far greater than any momentary struggle. We were living in the context of an eternal storyline God wrote for us –

and has written for all of us. Our Author joined us for a reason. He scripted a role we must play together – there's a purpose we can't fulfill separately. Ultimately, the intentionality with which I believe Erin and I were brought together was enough for me to commit to standing by her side forever, not knowing what storms we'll face along the way.

Have you ever had a major life-development creep up on you too quickly? Do you believe there was a purpose behind it? Have you discovered what that purpose is?

How Not to Hunt Deer

November 2016

- disappointing beginnings create happy endings -

The reality is the deeper the disappointment we feel in the moment, the more meaningful the long-term outcome is likely to be for us.

I couldn't wait for hunting season to roll around. Planning a wedding, incessantly traveling for work, organizing major life-changes. I balanced it all while living without a home as I considered the possibility of Erin and I moving to Denver instead of Washington D.C. (more on this in the next chapter). I don't do well when I'm trapped inside flying steel tubes and cement walls for extended periods of time, so the chance to be in the woods sans cellphone was more than exciting to me this hunting season. It was needed. However, deer season wouldn't be the soothing therapy for which I had hoped.

This fall, I'd learn that if our life stories were ultimately about us, and written by us, then we could control the outcomes. We could choose comfortable chapters and we could create favorable endings. But for the same reason that we'll never know how and when our stories end, we can't regulate the good and the bad in them. We must live through the uncertain, complex, and depressing chapters (and some of us to a greater extent than others) simply because we don't have a choice.

When we shift our perspective to see God as life's author, we gain a framework for understanding how disappointment, confusion, sadness, and frustration – the chapters we'd never choose for ourselves – shape us. You see, if authors don't stretch and develop their characters as the story progresses, the plot stagnates. Nobody reads a story about someone who goes to work, gets a positive performance review, returns home, eats dinner, sleeps, and does it all over again (even though we do this on a daily basis). We fall in love with the characters who face fear, doubt, adversity, and anxiety to become a better person by the final act.

Similarly, the start of my hunting season was marked by an initial moment of defeat that I would never have chosen for myself. By the end of my time in the woods, I realized that my early setback actually enabled me to live a more meaningful story – a story worth sharing.

––––

I walked into the farmhouse door and leaned my 12-gauge Benelli against the closet. I dropped the rest of my gear – my knife, rangefinder, gloves, extra slugs – onto the mudroom bench. I stripped down to my thermal leggings and walked into the kitchen. Erin and my mom were busy cooking dinner.

Lying on the ground with arms and legs sprawled, I moaned, "Ahhhh!"

"No luck, huh?" Erin guessed, peering over a pot of bubbling tomato sauce. She laughed as I lay prostrate on the oak floor.

"Worse. He was perfect. Ten points. Tall, wide, only 40 yards out," I sighed. "But I missed... twice. How do I miss from that range? I've made that shot with my bow, much less my shotgun!"

I raised and dropped my hands onto the log cabin's floor with open palms, reverberating a loud smack from the ceiling's tall trusses. I thought more sound effects would communicate my frustration more pointedly.

"I just don't get it," I continued rambling.

"Oh, I'm sorry sweets. That sounds frustrating," Erin frowned and tried to empathize as she stirred her sauce.

I usually loved hunting season. It didn't matter what season; bow or shotgun, deer or turkey. Hunting meant time with my dad. Growing up, the woods were the classroom and my dad the professor. He taught me to shoot, cut wood, and fix fence in the same trees where I had been hunting earlier that afternoon.

My dad coached me through taking my first doe when I was just 13 years old. His steady voice whispered the process from shouldering my shotgun, tracing the doe's walk, to squeezing off an even trigger-pull. His confidence and calm instruction were more memorable than actually taking my first deer with a long, 110-yard shot (that's a difficult shot with a shotgun slug, they don't travel as far and flat as a rifle).

When I left for college years later, I lived only two hours away from the farmhouse. I spent countless weekends there to get time alone. I liked working with my hands, being outside, and knowing I was beyond the reach of text messages and emails. It was a sanctuary of sorts. Deep breaths and smiles came easier at the farm.

I needed that feel-good on this particular weekend, but it never came. Instead, I felt strung-out and hopeless.

Hunting season always starts on a Friday morning. By Saturday afternoon, I was already lying on the kitchen floor in frustration. Friday night, Saturday morning, and Saturday afternoon had all presented an unprecedented number of shots at perfect trophy bucks – and I missed them all. Incredibly, I crossed paths with the same 10-point buck twice, as well as an equally impressive eight-pointer (it's very rare to get multiple shots at a buck in the same season, let alone ones that large). I squandered each chance. And when I say I missed, I mean *really* missed. I searched for a blood trail after each shot and despite spending two packs of slugs, I didn't find a single drop of blood.

If you've hunted before, you realize a few things. First, after every shot, a loud echo clangs throughout the woods, crackling into the ears of nearby hunters. Anyone within a mile of me would have known I took a shot. Second, when you hunt with a group, everyone walks home at sunset to find out who took what shots. It was embarrassing, quite frankly, to come up empty after so many shots. I knew I'd disappoint expecting faces.

A small part of me wanted to take a big buck just to impress Erin. I mean, "cave man bring home wild game to beautiful woman" crosses every guy's mind, right? Well, it does for the woodsy types, I suppose. Another part of me wanted to see my dad beaming as I drove in a big buck from the same woods where he first taught me to shoot an air rifle.

"How long are you going to lay there?" Erin wondered aloud.

"Until that buck walks into the backyard and I can grab my shotgun," I shot back. "But in all seriousness, probably another two minutes. I'm hungry." I just needed time to decompress.

———

Sunday's sunrise brought new hope that I'd have better luck. I geared up and was ready to head out to the field when Erin crept down the stairs to wish me luck.

"I bet you'll see something today, I can feel it," she whispered. She pulled back the camouflage bandana around my neck to kiss my lips for good luck.

"Thanks, love. I hope so," I said as I turned to the Jeep parked outside the farmhouse.

I drove south to a barn that houses the farm's steers. I parked next to its red paneling and felt the cold morning dew settle on my exposed skin as I swung open the Jeep's mud-splattered door. I watched my breath cloud in front of me before slinging my shotgun over my shoulder. Stuffing two boxes of shotgun shells into my vest, I set off on foot down the fence line. I cut west to the spur I had been set up in for the last two days. I figured that heck, if I had seen two bucks there, I might as well stay in the same area. If my shots were erratic, hopefully the deer trails would stay consistent.

A good size doe passed underneath my tree stand at first light. While this was no trophy buck, she would give us a good supply of venison. We'd be driving back to Chicago that night and my dad hadn't taken any shots, so I decided this was a good opportunity. We needed the meat. Besides, there was no way I could miss from only 10 yards away.

But I did miss. Again. I didn't even need to check for blood. The doe just trotted off, unhindered and glancing back to taunt me.

This was disturbing. I stared at my shotgun in disbelief. I felt confused more than anything. Even if I had lost my touch behind the scope (it had, in fact, been a while since I last shot) there was no real way to completely miss from a mere 10 yards. I climbed down from my tree immediately, incredulous. I couldn't stay there and take another shot only to miss yet again. I stormed back to the Jeep and sped to the farmhouse. There, I grabbed an oversize cardboard box that had encased a new 70-inch TV.

I stuck a set of bright orange targets to the box and propped up my makeshift target in an open field, exactly 50 yards from a collapsible shooting rest. After reloading my shotgun, I steadied myself on the rest to ensure I'd take an accurate shot. Then, I sent five rounds downrange.

I missed each shot. And I don't mean I missed the small orange targets. I missed the six-foot cardboard box entirely.

Slumping back from my shotgun, I felt a small wave of relief wash over me as I realized I wasn't the problem. I hadn't lost my touch. That relief quickly turned into intense frustration as it dawned on me that my scope had somehow been damaged. By extension, a whole weekend of hunting and an unheard-of number of shots at trophy bucks had just evaded me.

———

Like deer hunting, my life plans haven't always turned out as I've hoped. Can you relate to me here? Many times, frustrating circumstances that leave me with a hung head and swirling emotions are owed to no better reasons than faulty gear and a damaged scope.

On the other hand, with a clear reason, sense of purpose, and an end goal, it's quite amazing what types of physical and mental trials we're willing to endure. With a higher calling, a greater good, or an explicit reward at the end of it all, we throw ourselves into endurance races, 100-hour workweeks, and months of home improvement projects. We press forward knowing there's accomplishment, recognition, or financial gain waiting at the end of our pain. Afterward, we feel exhausted and spent, but also excited and satisfied.

But, can you imagine trying to endure a footrace while not knowing if you'll be racing for 10 or 100 miles? I can't. A finish line defines the race in every way. It informs training intensity, pacing, and how often to consume calories.

Knowing where the race ends is everything.

However, life doesn't give us a demarcated racecourse or a known finish line. We don't have that luxury. I think it's for the best, too. We'd lose a part of ourselves if life did play out like that – with every challenge presenting a clear purpose and a course map. While we'd gain a sense of certainty, immeasurable traits like perseverance, trust, and loyalty would have no place in our lives. If not for the defeating and confusing moments in my life – just like this particular hunting season – I wouldn't have built

built the same levels of faith and resolve I possess today.

The reality is that long-term plans are never revealed to us in the short term, and the deeper the disappointment we feel in the moment, the more meaningful the long-term outcome is likely to be for us. We will never have an omniscient knowledge of how our stories end. So, when we face failure, we do have to come up empty-handed, take a long drive home, and repair the damage (in this case, buy a new shotgun scope). But when we press forward and return to try again, we'll discover that our most rewarding triumphs are born from our ugliest trials.

———

Two weeks later, I was on a plane from D.C. to Chicago. I caught a cab from the airport to a café 30 miles south of the city. There, I bought a sandwich, met my dad in the parking lot, and we began our drive back to the farm for a final weekend of hunting. We didn't need the radio to keep us company. We talked for the entirety of the drive. It was refreshing. Stories of my dad meeting my mom, apologetics, family; we touched on a lot of topics like we always do.

"So, what do you think my chances are, realistically, of seeing that 10-pointer again?" I inquired.

My dad had spent more time at the farm during bow season, so I was curious to see if he had seen the same buck on other outings. Generally speaking, the bigger the buck, the more elusive he is. It takes time for deer to mature. If that 10-pointer had lived through multiple hunting seasons, he'd have surely learned to move away from the crack of gunfire. I figured my chances were slim-to-none after three consecutive days of missed shots, but I asked anyway.

"Well, if he likes a doe in that area, then he'll probably stick around. You do that for the right woman you know," my dad said with a grin.

I've always admired that. Thirty years later and he still beams whenever he talks about how madly in love with my mom he is. "I guess you're right," I laughed.

I was just hopeful that with a new scope in tow, I would see something big enough to give us venison for the year. Our family and friends love venison, so we usually try to hunt enough to gift or grill some for others. I wasn't expecting a trophy at this point.

"We'll know for sure soon enough."

———

"Did you see anything?" my dad asked as I walked into the farmhouse.

"Nope. I saw some doe about 200 yards out, near the ravine, but nothing after that. You?"

"About the same. A few small yearlings to the north. Too far, too small," he shrugged. "Let's eat."

It was Saturday morning which left Saturday afternoon and Sunday to find hunting success. I still had a chance, but I couldn't help feeling that fate wouldn't have anything different than missed shots in store for me.

"Eggs? Scrambled? How many?" I confirmed and got to work.

After eggs, a nap, coffee, and a few projects in the barn, I took some practice shots with my new scope. I clustered three consecutive shots inside of a two-inch circle. Pretty good. As we geared up shortly thereafter, I couldn't shake the nagging that I had just jinxed myself by wasting all the accurate shots I had left.

I decided to camp out in the same area I had been in all hunting season. I'd be inconsolable if I chose a new position and wound up watching that 10-pointer walk across my previous firing lane. I climbed my tree and loaded three shells into my shotgun. I was sweating from the long hike underneath all my warm layers. I could almost see faint wisps of steam as the warmth in my jacket rose to meet the frigid fall air. I stripped off my jacket, looped it around a branch, and settled in to wait.

The wind swayed the treetops in a slow dance and the sun's fading rays illuminated a cluster of golden leaves. As I watched nature's ballet, I felt an earnest prayer rise up within me.

"Lord, there's a whole lot happening right now. Erin and I are planning a wedding, I'm not sure if we'll land in D.C. or Denver, and I don't know what being a husband is like. You'll work it out,

I know that, but I'm not sure how. Would you remind me you're in control? That you'll provide for us?" I whispered to God.

I sat quietly for a few minutes before adding, "And could you give me a sign to share with Erin, please? I know you can give us peace or confidence, but would you give me something we can't misinterpret? Like that 10-pointer? Would you bring him back?"

A gnawing feeling began to intensify inside me. It swayed me like the trees in the wind, yo-yoing me from a sense of trust in God's provision to doubt He was actually listening. And even if He were listening, does God really give tangible signs like that?

The sun slipped below the tree line. I tried to not let it drag my sense of hope down with it. "He'll provide," I reminded myself.

I saw the first buck before I heard him. He was quiet. Years of roaming the woods taught him to move slowly across an exposed field. Three hundred yards out, beyond my range, the smaller eight-pointer I had seen during the previous weekend crept beyond the wood line. I held my breath as he scanned the field. While he wasn't the taller 10-point buck, this was it.

I shouldered my shotgun and centered my scope over the kill zone. As I traced his walk in my crosshairs, he started to close the gap between us. It was a complete tossup as I waited. If he chose to move in any direction but due north, I couldn't confidently attempt a shot. He would remain outside of my range. There was just enough daylight left for me to wait for him to draw closer.

I heard a discreet snapping noise and I looked up from my scope. There, looking out from a break in the woods, stood the exact same majestic 10-point buck. He was back! My heart raced as he surveyed the field. "No. Way." I gasped.

Both bucks were in the same field. The 10-pointer followed the eight-pointer heading due north. Soon, both had drawn within 80 and 60 yards from me, respectively.

The 10-pointer was obviously my first choice of the two. It was pretty much a certainty that the eight-pointer would scatter after the crack of my first shot so I eased my shotgun's muzzle toward the 10-pointer. Centering my scope's crosshairs, I tuned into the rise and fall of my heaving chest and I calmed my breathing. After another second passed, I squeezed the trigger.

SNAP! My shot rang out, bellowing through the foliage.

The buck leapt high into the air and tore off beyond the ridgeline at the opposite edge of the field. I remained locked behind my scope, trying to track the buck's scramble to safety. He vanished into the woods in a two-second disappearing act. He was gone, so I curiously scanned the field to see where the second buck had run.

Amazingly, the eight-pointer had only run 15 yards. He was standing frozen in the field, attempting to locate me. I dropped my crosshairs onto his chest and I paused just long enough to mentally process my next move. My dad hadn't taken any shots, and I knew we needed the meat. I quieted my adrenaline-fueled breathing and refocused. Then, I squeezed off a second shot.

CRACK! A second hit! He kicked up his hind legs and bolted toward the same wood line, crashing through the trees in another split second. The whole sequence unfolded inside of 10 seconds. While my dad would have heard the shots, they were so close together he would likely assume I was putting a finishing shot into the same deer. Quickly, I slipped my phone out of my vest pocket and called him.

"Dad," I whispered. "Don't shoot anything. I took two bucks, and I know I hit them both. They were the exact same guys as last weekend."

"Unbelievable," he mused, equally shocked as excited.

"I'm going to wait until last light to look for blood. I'll text you what I find so you can grab the Jeep afterward."

"Okay, sounds good sonny boy," he confirmed and hung up.

I sank back against the tree's ridged bark. It wasn't over. I still had to confirm and recover both bucks. Even so, God had provided to a miraculous degree. The sign I prayed for showed up within minutes. And not only was it the same buck, there were two of them. God had answered my prayer in grand fashion as if to remind me, "While you'll be the husband soon, I still control the story. I'll provide."

I ejected the last shell from my shotgun's chamber and I climbed down from the tree. My fingers tingled with a mix of adrenaline and anticipation as my boots hit the soil with a soft thud. Daylight was fading and I still needed to trace a blood trail. Two blood trails, actually. I strapped on my headlight to start my search. The ground was cold enough that I could move quickly over the frozen terraces without sinking into soft dirt.

Tracking the 10-pointer's trail first, I moved toward an opening in the woods. Soon enough, I found a line of leaves painted bright red and leading me into a ravine. It was a kill shot; only the vitals could have colored the leaves so vividly. This guy was smart, too. He had nestled himself into a thicket of briars in the least accessible part of the wooded gulch.

I couldn't believe it. It was a perfect shot. He would have been in shock until he faded. A clean kill (for reference, if you're wondering how a buck that runs off is considered a "clean kill," deer always have enough energy to run off while in shock, and without pain). I draped my vest over a neighboring tree to mark his position. Then I maneuvered my way through the thorns and back to the top of the ridge.

I tapped out a short message to my dad after finding cell service again. "Found the big guy. Will need some tow straps and the Jeep – he's deep. Going to look for the next."

I dropped to one knee, breathing a little easier. Equal parts gratitude and amazement swept over me as I whispered, "God, don't let me forget this night. When we don't see the reason behind something, help Erin and I remember you've got us."

I decided to search for the second buck before texting Erin. I wanted to tell her the full story. I walked back to where he had kicked up the earth and found faint drops of blood. Tracing them into the same ravine, I discovered I had made another clean shot. The second buck had landed just 50 yards north of the first.

"Can you bring a second knife?" I texted my dad before pulling up my conversation with Erin to text her, "Good news. I'll call you later."

———

"It's good to hear your voice, love," I told Erin as I laid in bed. "Ready for a story?"

I recounted the night's events for her. I shared how strongly I felt this hunting season was far more significant than a trophy buck. We talked about how God had provided in the past, and we committed to trusting that He would continue to do so in our married life.

"I'm glad you can do the hunting stuff," Erin said. "We're a good team. But you'll always come home to me after, right?" Erin knew the answer, but she needed me to repeat it.

"Always, E. I'll always come back to you."

"You know," I continued, "I was so disappointed last weekend. I was just so down in the moment. But I think that's why I feel so grateful now. This night feels so much sweeter having passed through all the frustration, first."

"Totally," Erin agreed. "For me too."

I could almost hear her smile over the phone.

Couches, Sleeping Bags & Wedding Plans (Part 1)

December 2016

- your deepest joys must be found outside yourself -

If we find ourselves with a desire that nothing in this world
can satisfy, the most probable explanation is that we
were made for another world. – C.S. Lewis

———————

Engagement was a strange dichotomy of both exhaustion and exhilaration. I considered myself to be married for all intents and purposes at this point, because after proposing, at least in my mind, I had committed to spending my life with Erin. That's what a wedding is all about, right? And yet, I wasn't married. Erin and I weren't living together, and I spent countless sleepless nights traveling to see her, planning our wedding, and building our new life together.

I was living through the most thrilling yet tiring season of my life. My nonstop travel collided with the facts that: one, I had no clue where we'd be moving after the wedding (Washington D.C., Chicago, and Denver were all possibilities at this stage); two, I felt mounting pressure to perform at work while leading the chase to the company's revenue goal; and three, I was living on friends' couches and futons because my loft had become too expensive and impractical to keep.

Essentially, I lived as a modern nomad for eight months. I moved from couches to futons with a bright green duffel bag, a sleeping bag, and my laptop in tow. I rarely stayed in one place for more than a handful of days, and I didn't always know where I'd land next. According to Southwest Airlines, I boarded 63 flights during just six months in this chapter of my life. The air miles added up quickly as I worked in D.C., visited Erin and my family in Chicago, and traveled to our future home in Denver (where we ultimately landed two months after our wedding).

So, how did Denver enter the mix? After our company's move to Washington D.C., Denver became a possible city as Erin and I considered our new life together. We wanted to be known together as "Erin and Nate" in a new community. Leaving Chicago for a season meant the ability to carve out a new identity as a team, a unit. Denver fit our lifestyle, too. Our company was also expanding west, and I'd need to continue traveling for work, so I proposed the flexibility to leave D.C. for Denver. They agreed.

Life on-the-go was an energizing adventure at first, but a draining chore by the end of it all. I usually stayed on the couch of an Airbnb that Brian (founder-Brian from earlier in the story) had rented in D.C. Like me, he lived a pretty itinerant life during those months. The normalcy of having a kitchen and hallways felt more restful than sterile hotel rooms to us. On Fridays and weekends, I'd accept whatever accommodations were offered to me. My favorite place was Greg's futon. He bought an extra-foam mattress pad, just so I'd have a comfortable stay when I visited.

———

After Travis (my other colleague, who raced with the flat tire earlier in the story) joined Brian in D.C. full-time, we concurred that booking the same Airbnb for a few months in a row would give them the chance to look for permanent apartments, while allowing me to leave my clothes in one place as I came and went. It was a solid plan in theory. Trouble arose, however, when I discovered that the "third bed" described in the listing was nothing more than another pullout couch – and it didn't pull out.

"Crap."

I cursed the couch as I tugged against its frame, attempting to coax the mess of bent rails into unfurling. Brian and I had a streak of good fortune during the past four months, discovering relatively comfortable accommodations at decent prices. The pullout couches I slept on were always restful and easy to manage. That streak of luck skidded to an abrupt stop as I stared down at this particular couch through a fog of jetlag. Its thin, wafer-like mattress was tangled between twisted metal support rails that looked more like spaghetti noodles than a solid frame.

I was frustrated, weary, and my 3:30 a.m. wakeup call had shortened my fuse. The strain of constant transit and transition weighed on me more heavily these days. Even if I could have wrenched the pullout's rails back into proper form, I wasn't certain it would support me for the night. So, I jerked the folded mattress (if you could even call it that) from the couch and dropped it onto the floor.

I reached into my loyal green duffel bag and pulled out a dear friend, my sleeping bag, from its compression sack. Those 78 inches of blue and grey nylon felt like home to me. Even after we were married, Erin had to talk me out of curling up inside of it on our couch, for old time's sake. I folded my sweatshirt around a couch cushion to create a makeshift pillow and I slipped the sleeping bag's zippers around my head, mummy-style.

I texted Erin goodnight as I listened to the pitter-patter of rain drops smacking the roof. The rain's noise was augmented by drops falling into a bucket positioned a few feet from my head, catching what our leaking roof couldn't. As I awaited Erin's reply, I considered my options. I'd have to clean up twice the mess if the bucket overflowed in the middle of the night, but I had little desire to get up and empty it. I was already enveloped in a warm sleeping bag with no motivation to change that.

I studied the bucket once more after Erin texted me back. As I considered my next move, falling asleep or dumping the bucket, I spotted a mouse scurrying across the floor at my eyelevel. A streetlamp cast an orange arc through the living room, spotlighting the little guy's midnight run. He (maybe she?) scuttled across the wet tile and vanished behind a loose baseboard near the front door.

I couldn't help but laugh. I expected to groan at the nuisance, lamenting the nights – and weeks – ahead with rodents for roommates. Somehow, I felt grateful. I was actually thankful for our little houseguest. It just felt right, as if mice were fitting for my current condition. Besides, I might as well have some company on the floor, right?

A flood of joy quickly swept over me. In the moment, I felt that a sleeping bag, a 98 percent intact roof, and my journey toward marriage were all the comforts I needed. A smile spread across my face as I settled into a just-right groove between my sweatshirt and the couch cushion. I cherished the grin hanging between my cheekbones for a few minutes, reflecting on how gratitude, when surrounded by abundance and excess, is such a fleeting emotion. Stripping away my 800-thread-count sheets and a waterproof roof actually stoked, not stifled, gratitude.

The truth was that I was sleeping on the ground out of great privilege and blessing. Although my sleeping conditions were worse than my normal futon or blow-up mattress, I was living through one of my most fruitful chapters. I was waiting to marry the love of my life. I held an elevated position in a growing company, and I found my work fulfilling. I enjoyed being on the road, and I was saving for mortgage payments. Leaky roof aside, things were looking up.

———

My temptation that night was to focus on my exhaustion. To grumpily complain that my circumstances could have been better. That's the great deceit of our surroundings, isn't it? They're brilliant liars. They're well-versed in distracting us from the big picture and preventing us from living as part of the broader narrative.

It would have been very easy to overlook the storyline unfolding in parallel to my immediate surroundings, you see. As I gained a wife and a growing career, God was making me into a more whole, healthy person. He was asking me to bear my trying conditions to ready me for leadership in marriage and business.

The reality is that our surroundings can always be better. They can be different, at the very least. They're always shifting and never absolute. If we accept this, we can also accept that any happiness rooted solely in our immediate context is cheap. To be clear, I'm not suggesting circumstantial happiness is inherently bad. What I am saying, is if we always build our lives on cut-rate, discount happiness, one storm is all it takes to knock us down.

What we need is a more solid, unwavering contentment that transcends the immediate good and bad in our lives. Finding joy in a source outside of what we can manufacture for ourselves, outside of our careers or accomplishments, for example, will cement a pure and incorruptible joy within us.

That's what's backward. True joy – something we all crave – cannot come from within us. It must originate far above and outside us. When we live aligned with this truth, and we accept the reality that we can't self-generate the deeply satisfying kind of happiness we desire, our ability to soak up the "little" joys in life actually increases.

When we're no longer leaning on impressive houses, new cars, standout skills, remarkable résumés, people's perceptions, exotic vacations, or other momentary fillers, and we begin to derive our meaning, purpose, and fulfillment in a storyline that transcends anything we could ever produce on our own, we're then free to enjoy the little things of life.

Ravi Zacharias, an apologist who's lived the majority of his life on the road, teaching everyone from students to world leaders, found the Christian faith while laying on a hospital bed after a failed suicide attempt. Speaking from experience, he raises an interesting consideration about finding lasting joy:

> God's made you for a purpose, and all the tiny little purposes become purposeful because your life itself has purpose. If you

don't have ultimate purpose, all these tiny little purposes are just ways of tranquilizing your boredom. God's given you an ultimate calling - meaning, meaning, meaning.[xvii]

You can see Mr. Zacharias' point in an athlete who competes to support a teammate's victory, a soldier who selflessly protects a squad mate, or an entrepreneur who creates something for the good of others. Each labors for a purpose far greater than themselves. If you ask why they agree to tolerate ruthless hours, uncertain outcomes, and intense stressors, they'll tell you they are most fulfilled when their own happiness isn't the end goal.

The trouble begins, however, after the championship is won, the battle is over, and the work is retired. What's next? Where's the ultimate fulfillment that doesn't compel you to continue chasing it? While sure, there may be another season, war, or career to choose, we all die one day. What will come at the end of it all? If everything simply disappears after death, where's the true, lasting joy? Where's the "big" meaning in life on this Earth?

This is what Mr. Zacharias calls into question when he refers to an "ultimate calling," which brings, "meaning, meaning, meaning." When you find ultimate purpose in a story that's bigger than your own, the chapters within your story – maybe it's building a company, serving in the armed forces, or competing athletically – all shift from a seasonal to an eternally satisfying pleasure.

———

Tom Brady gave us a textbook case study of this.

He was featured on CBS' *60 Minutes* after winning his third Super Bowl. He was 27 years old and he had just signed a record-setting NFL contract with the New England Patriots. Somehow, in the midst of it all, he felt something was missing. Despite what culture told him was the ultimate achievement – becoming a champion, multimillionaire quarterback married to a swimsuit model – he found it cheap. He was disturbingly unsatisfied. He told the reporter:

> Why do I have three Super Bowl rings and still think there's something greater out there for me? I mean, maybe a lot of people would say, 'Hey man, this is what it is.' I reached my goal, my dream, my life [but] I think, 'God, it's got to be more than this.' I mean this can't be what it's all cracked up to be. I mean I've done it. I'm 27. And what else is there for me?[xviii]

I think Tom Brady would have an incredibly stimulating dinner conversation with Paul, the apostle from the Bible. Paul wrote a letter to his friends in an ancient town called Philippi. He sat in shackles, imprisoned for sharing stories of Jesus as he composed one of history's most enlightening sets of instructions on how to find joy. Paul knew what he was talking about, too. He befriended hardship. He flirted with adversity. He had been shipwrecked, beaten, stoned, mocked, imprisoned, and brought to the point of death on multiple occasions before writing his letter. And yet, as Paul awaited news of when and how he would be executed by the Roman government, he was able to write this:

> I have learned to be content whatever the circumstances. I know what it is to be in need, and I know what it is to have plenty. I have learned the secret of being content in any and every situation, whether well fed or hungry, whether living in plenty or in want. I can do all this through *him* who gives me strength. [xix]

So, what was at the top of Paul's how-to-find-joy instructions list? Community to be certain, but more so, Paul said the source of his joy was rooted in his Creator. He said he found strength and contentment for *all* circumstances by looking to someone who is far greater than himself – God.

Can you imagine Paul showing up in a toga to have dinner with Tom Brady on the terrace of a Boston mansion? It'd make for a great follow-up *60 Minutes* episode. I'd pay to serve as the waiter for that meal. Paul would most likely first muse at the concept of rosemary chicken and walnut spinach salads at first, but once he overcame his fascination with modern food, I think these two characters would produce the greatest dialogue in the history of *60 Minutes*.

"Paul, help me out with that letter you wrote to your friends. Connect the dots for me. Did you ever see that interview I did?"

"Oh yes, these things called 'TVs' are crazy. Nobody uses

parchment to document things anymore."

"Well, what gives? I've looked for joy everywhere there is to look in this world - sports, fame, mansions, pretty women, everywhere! And I'll tell you what, it's not here. So, tell me your secret, and I'll teach you to throw a tight 50-yard spiral."

To make this scene even more epic, imagine C.S. Lewis walking into the room to add to Paul and Tom's discussion, *"If we find ourselves with a desire that nothing in this world can satisfy, the most probable explanation is that we were made for another world."*[xx]

———

I wonder if life was easier when Paul was alive. Not the persecution, stoning, and shipwreck parts. I just figure the pace of life was slower then. Much of my challenge is the immediacy and speed with which I think I need to live. If Paul traveled by foot, made his own tents, and kneaded his own bread, he probably didn't feel much hurry in life. He probably had more free moments than he cared for while sitting in jail.

I still prefer my story to build and rise quickly. When things aren't moving fast enough, I begin to bounce my legs in agitation and I'm consumed by my own thoughts. Erin says I can have conversations with myself in a crowded room. My thoughts roll on and I get sucked into the bliss or despair or whatever the moment brings me into for a short while. I neglect the lessons

I've learned, which can rescue me from the storm of my present thoughts if I only had the mindfulness to recall them.

I often believe what I feel in the moment is the whole truth. On this particular night, however, a thin mattress, an echoing bucket, and a small mouse reminded me of the lasting joy we can find through our world's Big Story, and I slept easy.

Couches, Sleeping Bags & Wedding Plans (Part 2)

December 2016

- your deepest joys must be found outside yourself -

Those eyes man, those aren't your eyes. I have the same ones.
They're dead, they're tired. The life's not in them.

―――――――――

"How are you?" soon became a loaded question. A certain expectation accompanied it. Arguably, Erin and I were living through the most enthralling season of our lives. So, for good reason, most people assumed we were simply floating above the ground, waiting to get married and move our little family to a beautiful city in the mountains.

I felt deceitful if I replied with a canned line of, "Great, life's really good right now." Like I was hiding behind a smokescreen. But confessing how strung-out I was while living out of two small bags just wasn't a feasible response, either. My chest would tighten and my mind shut down, attempting to fend off anxiety.

The gravity of how poorly I was processing everything set in when Erin and I were at a welcome-back party for a good friend, Ryan. Ryan was playing professional hockey and his team came into town to play the Chicago Blackhawks. Everyone had gathered at his family's house to wish him luck.

I used to ride the bench during high school baseball games as Ryan would circle the bases, making the sport seem easy. I'd pass the time by inventing little games with sunflower seeds and water cups while he was on the field. Because we spent our summers together, taking road trips and just living life alongside each other, he knows me well. He can read me. Generally, I keep my cards close and I like to ask the questions to control the conversation. Ryan pierces right through that veil, however.

He has an exceptional sensitivity to what people are thinking, even in group settings. While in a room of nine people doing four different activities, he can point out what everyone is talking about or feeling. I don't think it's always conscious; it's just inside him. That awareness is even more precise around me, given our history.

I stuck to the corner of the room at his welcome-home party, introducing Erin to someone I knew from the baseball team years ago. I was thankful for a reason to avoid small talk with other people. I was skirting the "How are you?" question. There must have been 50 people there, so Erin and I hung around until the crowd thinned to talk with Ryan for more than a minute.

As people filtered out the front door, Ryan turned to me and said, "Those eyes man, those aren't your eyes."

It caught me off guard.

"I have the same ones. They're dead. They're tired, the life's not in them," he repeated as I searched for my words.

I wasn't ready to acknowledge that I was strung out. I wouldn't come to terms with how spent I actually was until weeks later, when I broke down after picking Erin up from her bridal shower. I walked into a room with three long tables full of gifts. Having lived with just a pair of jeans and a sleeping bag for quite some time at that point, I was downright overwhelmed by the amount of stuff. I crumpled after we left.

My chest tightened as I stared back at Ryan with hollow eyes.

I was quiet as I drove back into the city. Too quiet for Erin's liking. I was still ruminating on Ryan's words, "They're dead. They're tired, the life's not in them." How had he known? We hadn't exchanged a lot of words, but they weighed on me as heavily as an hour-long late-night conversation. Those words felt heavier because I hadn't yet told Erin how spent I actually was. I didn't want her to worry about the tightening in my chest. I figured that cluing her in would just cause her more stress. She'd assume I was having serious heart issues or something. Besides, she was under enough stress of her own.

How could it be that during the supposed most-happy season

of my life, I was just a shell of myself, with my body physically manifesting the mental exhaustion I felt? I didn't believe my story was supposed to work like that. So, I did what I had trained myself to do. I smiled, said it was good to see Ryan, and carried along hiding it from Erin.

———

Weeks later, I pulled open the Uber app on my phone as I strode past gate B10 at Midway Airport. I knew I'd pass the sandwich shop in one minute, and within another four, I'd be outside the main terminal to catch my ride home. I had my travel down to a science. My ride's wait time said five minutes, but the driver would show up in seven, giving me just enough time to make a pit stop in the bathroom, power walk up the ramp, and slide into the car without waiting in Chicago's bitter winter air.

My spot on the floor back in D.C. wasn't so bad. I thought I might actually miss sleeping there one day. Besides, it was almost Christmas. Soon, I'd be in Vail sharing the bunk bed – a real bed – with my brother for the holidays.

I hopped into my taxi and zoned out for the 40-minute trip to the north side of the city. I had learned better – if I cracked open my laptop and started on emails or projects, I'd lose my mind to that activity for the night. I'd stay on the mental track I put myself on, which wasn't fair to Erin. We'd been waiting over a week to see each other.

I took Erin's stairs two at a time and I knocked on her second-floor door. I pictured her smile as I waited. I had seen that "Nate's home" smile many times, but I loved seeing it each and every time. On the weeks that I was riding some career high and I didn't want to leave D.C., that smile called me home. I knew, even if I wanted to, I couldn't stay in the capitol. Someone loved me very much back home.

There it was. Erin's smile spread across pretty white teeth and below two perfect, almond-shaped brown eyes that welled up, as if to say our joy should have as much sparkle as our sadness. Like she always did, she bit her lip, laughed a little, and grabbed her hands to keep them occupied. She was giving me enough time to drop my bag before shooting her arms around me in a bear hug.

I smiled, "It's good to see you E." I stepped into the apartment and dropped my bag in its home. I had a system. I'd position my duffel so it didn't block Erin or her roommate, Tiffany (who became one of my favorite roommates during this season), from walking in or out, while giving me easy access from the couch.

After a hug, the 30-second kind of hug where you breathe easier by the end of it, I walked into the kitchen and sat on the counter. It usually takes me some time to adjust to being home. Slowing down is a process for me, but I was ready this night. I was ready to be home, to see Erin, and to make dinner together. I helped her slice brussels sprouts before she dusted them with spices and slid them into their 400-degree tomb.

As I walked to the living room and sank into the couch, the feeling of home swept over me. In this season, "home" simply felt like the cessation of motion to me. The sensation spellbound me for a few minutes. I lied on the couch, gazing up at the ceiling, wondering if I could articulate what home felt like to Erin as she walked into the room. I didn't have an actual mailing address yet, so home didn't feel like the most appropriate word. Perhaps I was feeling certain. Maybe, despite not knowing where I'd sleep that weekend (let alone what city we'd sleep in once married), I felt certain I was supposed to be starting a life with Erin.

It was curious that in a season where the small things of life – where I'd sleep or how I'd spend my hours – were all unknown until the hour they were brought to me, I was positively certain of the big things. I was marrying Erin, we were starting a life together, and we were moving cities. My day-to-day was by far the most shaken and unclear it had ever been, but my Author knew how our story would work out. I just had to keep living forward, appreciating how I was maturing in the process.

Bunk Beds and Beaches (Part 2)

June 2017

- we lose something in the process of gaining something -

I just want to have a day where you trust me enough to step
out of what's familiar and come on an adventure.
That's all. I just want one big adventure.

We lean in a little closer when our favorite characters encounter difficult choices. We can't help it. We need to know what happens next. We're hooked until we discover how things turn out. Does the plot twist off course? How did we not see that coming?

Choices are strategic elements in a story. They're used to signal plot shifts and measure character growth. Authors weave them into the critical moments of all kinds of stories – even those as goofy and lovable as *Elf*.

Have you seen *Elf*? If so, you know that Buddy the Elf decides to move from the North Pole to New York City in order to find his long-lost father, Walter. However, unbeknownst to Buddy, Walter also has another son, Michael. Once Buddy locates Walter, he and Michael become fast-friends. They bond over the fact that their father is a workaholic and selfishly consumed by his ambition as a book publisher, rarely taking time off to enjoy his family. Toward the end of *Elf*, Buddy runs away from home. Michael, scared of what might happen to Buddy, begs Walter to help him search for his brother. In Michael's moment of panic, Walter is in the middle of pitching a career-defining book idea to the publishing company's owner, Mr. Greenway.

In the opening scene of the movie, we believe the crux of the story is whether or not Buddy will find his father in a massive, unknown city. As the story develops, and after Buddy locates Walter, we find ourselves craving to see them reconnect emotionally, as father and son. Buddy found Walter, but he didn't find his father. Walter is wholly unengaged with, and even annoyed by, the emergence of his long-lost son. He's still agitated when Michael comes bursting into the boardroom during his big presentation to ask him to search for Buddy.

In that moment, Walter is faced with a choice. Will he choose his career and continue to be a disengaged, disinterested father? Or will Walter risk his personal ambition to gain something much greater – his family's admiration? Here's how the scene unfolds:

[Walter making his pitch] Now, just picture this...

Michael: Dad! I gotta talk to you.

Walter: Michael, what is it?

Michael: Buddy ran away. He... he left a note. I'm scared, dad, he's gone.

Walter: Uh, let me just finish this meeting, and then, um, we'll figure it out.

Michael: Figure out what?! Buddy cares about everybody. All you care about is yourself.

Walter: Hey, Michael. Wait. We're gonna have to reschedule this, uh, Mr. Greenway.

Mr. Greenway: We don't have time to reschedule. I wanna hear the damn thing now. Son, you'll have to wait.

Walter: No, d-don't tell my kid what to do, uh...Can't... can't we do this another time, Mr. Greenway?

Mr. Greenway: I flew in just to hear this pitch, and I intend to.

Walter: It's gonna have to wait.

Mr. Greenway: If you wanna keep your job Walter Hobbs, you will pitch me this book right now!

Walter: Well... up yours.

Michael: Yeah, up yours!

Mr. Greenway: Hobbs... Hobbs! Hobbs, you walk out of here, and... and you're finished at Greenway! You're finished![xxi]

You see, Walter's choice not only serves as a stake in the ground, measuring how he's matured throughout the movie, it signals resolution to the story's central conflict. As Walter and Michael stride out of the boardroom, we're hopeful that Buddy will reconnect with his father. We sense they'll soon rekindle their lost sense of family. Then, we clap, cheer, and celebrate as the story concludes with Walter and Buddy reconnecting.

———

I made the right choice as I laid in those bunk beds, one year prior. Despite the wrestling match that pitted me against my own thoughts while I considered proposing to Erin, deep down, I knew I had met my person. I truly believed marriage would be more fulfilling than a life spent alone. Nonetheless, it was challenging to give up the freedom and autonomy I enjoyed in my former single life. To be honest, it's still a tough choice. To this day, whenever Erin and I aren't communicating well, it's usually because I've allowed my independence to drive a temporary wedge between us.

Generally speaking, I've found that men will empathize with this tug-of-war between meaningful relationships and selfish independence to a more acute degree. But isn't it true that all of us, in all areas of life, want to figure out how to have it both ways? We want the new and good things that require sacrifice to attain, but we just want the gain without the loss. We don't like tradeoffs.

We don't appreciate choices.

Looking back, I should have embraced the discomfort I was feeling on those bunk beds. I should have taken more time to study why I felt as I did. If only I had fully absorbed what God was teaching me then, I'd have been equipped for the same lesson to come right back 'round 10 months later. This time, the reality that I can't have it both ways rudely confronted me in the South of Thailand. On our honeymoon, no less.

In the time that elapsed between this particular day and the morning I contemplated proposing, Erin and I got married and moved to Denver. Throughout the process, I kept a closed-fisted grip on my time and interests while simultaneously attempting to cultivate a healthy marriage. I was blind to the duality of expecting a rewarding life with my wife while concurrently clinging to my past life.

Frankly, I had some growing up to do. It's obvious, even to those who aren't married, that healthy relationships don't blossom by prioritizing your interests over your significant other's. Although I'd had enough opportunities to learn this five times over, I suppressed those experiences as I sat on a pristine, white-sand beach. They buzzed like mosquitoes in my ear, reminding me I was heading for trouble, but I simply swatted them away.

There were early signs of trouble-in-paradise during the first week of our honeymoon. I was constantly venturing away on my own to rock climb, swim out to sea, or explore what lay beyond our hiking trail. At the same time, I was attempting to maintain the appearance of engaging in Erin's preferred activities. Having it both ways – my own adventure and a shared experience – was not actually possible, however.

My duplicitous strategy worked out so that I either missed the chance to connect with Erin because I was too focused on my own interests, or we spent time together, but I was too distracted for it to be truly meaningful.

Had I stopped to consider that I'm only a small part of the Big Story, I'd have learned from the greatest choice history has ever witnessed. In the turning point of our world's story, God sends his Son, Jesus, to die on a cross. Not only that, but Jesus actually chooses to go through with it. And while these choices did afford us life, love, and grace, tremendous sacrifice, bloodshed, and torment accompanied them.

Bottom line? I wanted my way. I wanted to control our story. I desired a full life with Erin, but without the required sacrifice. It wasn't fair to Erin, and it wound up frustrating me.

———

So, how did part two of the bunk-bed lesson continue on a beach in Thailand? The story really starts on Thanksgiving Day, during the fall before our trip. Erin and I were planning our honeymoon over a game of cards. I don't recall if Erin tasked me with planning the honeymoon or if I insisted I own it, but in any event, I was in charge of crafting our trip.

We readily agreed Thailand would be our destination. Neither of us had traveled to Asia, and we both felt it offered the right blend of food, culture, and nature. We also agreed to depart after we had settled into our new home in Denver, which would happen after our February wedding date. That meant June was the ideal date, so I booked our flights while dealing the cards.

I remember asking Erin in between hands of Gin, "What are your must-haves for this trip?" She didn't want to spend the entirety of our trip in the rainforest, and she wanted to end the trip on a relaxing note. Adventure at the beginning, massages and beaches at the end. I felt that was a reasonable request. While I skew toward sleeping in hostels and eating food from roadside carts, that's not exactly a recipe for romanticism.

Compromise felt equitable as we planned, but unjustly restrictive once we arrived in Thailand. So, I did what all good husbands do. I tossed our consensus out the window.

I suppose I was just overtaken by the awesomeness of a new country. I saw opportunity in all of our surroundings. I wanted to climb trees, jump into rivers, and sleep under bug nets. I was like Ralphie from *A Christmas Story*, mesmerized by the Red Rider BB Gun, gawking at its potential.

Now, reading this after the fact, you might be feeling, "What in the world was Nate thinking? He's talking about his honeymoon here, right? And he was frustrated his wife didn't want to sleep in the jungle?"

Yep, still talking about the honeymoon. If you Google "Railay Beach," you'll see what I'm referring to. You'll likely recognize the iconic rock formations that create the bookends to Railay. They're painted on almost every postcard and travel commercial that depicts white sands, clear waters, and beautiful tropics. It's as amazing in person as it looks in the pictures, too. As an ever-adventurer, the beach's beauty fueled my craving for a bold new expedition. And because that craving had intensified during two weeks of travel before arriving at Railay, it was darn close to Category-4-hurricane strength as we pick up the story.

———

"Why does it take me so much longer to get out of the house?" Erin paced around our villa, looking to see if she had missed packing sunscreen, glasses, or extra clothes.

I shrugged, "I don't know. Guess you're just needy?" I joked. "Tell me how to help."

I picked up a black raincoat, "Here, I have your raincoat. What else do you need?"

"Umm, can you grab those shorts sitting on the pool chair? We should bring them inside. We can't leave them out for the day." Erin motioned toward the sliding glass door.

"Oh, I'm sure they're fine. Let's go," I reassured her.

It was our second-to-last full day in Thailand. Soon, we'd be heading back to Bangkok, Tokyo, and then on to Denver. I was feeling antsy. I wanted to make the most of our final days away.

While we had already visited Bangkok, Chiang Mai, Phuket, and Krabi, I wanted more. Erin, by contrast, was feeling more worn down as the trip progressed. She'd been traveling for two weeks in a new culture, changing cities right as she began to settle into any particular place, and she was excited to relax on the beach for a change (which I agreed to while planning our trip).

We were starting the day on opposite extremes. Later, this would produce the perfect storm.

"Okay, I think I have everything. Let's go!" Erin ran past me and jumped outside, just to ask, "Aren't you coming? You're kind of slow in the mornings, huh?"

I laughed and locked our door, flipping the keys along their ring until I found one for the scooter. The owner of our villa was nice enough to let us borrow it. We could get anywhere in the peninsula we needed without paying for taxis or searching for parking. Erin rolled open the gate to our compound as I rocked the scooter back and forth. The owner said we'd have to jiggle the engine to life. Sure enough, it started up on my fifth shake.

We set off down the winding dirt roads and I navigated into the downtown's main strip. I parked us near a little hut selling long-tail boat tickets. To access Railay Beach, you have to catch a water taxi by showing the boat owners a little pink slip, which they can redeem for cash at the ticket hut. Each boat is a narrow, colorful wooden ship with twin tips that jut out above the water.

They look like smaller versions of those boats Vikings used to sail. They're driven by Thai captains who navigate 10-foot long poles with exposed propellers in and out of the water. The poles are fastened to an old diesel engine that's propped up by two-by-four planks, and yes. It looks just as sketchy as it sounds.

I bought two roundtrip slips of paper and held them up for Erin to see. "Okay! We got our tickets. This guy says the boats leave from a pier about a half mile that way. It's high-tide right now, so the boats have to go out of that pier instead of this one."

"Yeah, I just talked with this shuttle driver," Erin pointed to a truck with a row of benches in the back bed. "He said they shuttle people who bought tickets down to the other pier. I think we should go with them."

I looked at the shuttle and saw a family with three squirming children crawling around the seats. They looked like ants who'd found a picnic table with raspberry jam smeared all over the tablecloth. I looked back at Erin, confused. "Why would we want to do that? If we know the pier is that way, why don't we just take the scooter? We won't have to wait for anyone."

I understood where Erin was coming from, but it frustrated me. While I'd never actually traveled to the pier before, I was confident I could figure out how to get there. Erin, on the other hand, wanted to have a local drive us. She didn't want to risk the chance we'd wander around in an unknown city, lost and searching for something we had been offered a free ride to.

I was restless. I wanted to get moving instead of waiting for an undetermined number of people to load into the truck. As far as I was concerned, we were free people with the key to our scooter. Discovering our path would pacify my impatience, and it was all part of the day's fun.

"Nate, it's safer to go with these people. They'll take us right to the pier and we'll get to the beach eventually." Erin stepped toward the truck, beckoning for me to follow.

She wasn't smiling. She was serious. She did not want to get on our scooter.

"Fine," I caved, rolling my eyes and dragging myself to the truck as if I had been assigned some insurmountable task.

We piled into the corner of the truck and waited in the sun for a few minutes. I grew quiet, occupying myself by smacking flies that landed on the truck's banana-yellow paint. We waited for a few more couples to filter into the truck's bed before its engine rumbled to life.

As we drove toward the pier, Erin studied me. "What's the deal? Why are you so salty all of a sudden? Because we're not taking the scooter?"

"Yeah, I mean no," I started to explain. "I just want you to trust that I can actually get us there. I mean, look where we are. We'd already be out on the water right now."

"But we lost all of what, 15 minutes? Tops?" Erin probed, still confused as to why I wasn't happy.

"Okay. Sure."

I didn't want to continue the conversation. My short fuse stemmed from my own shortcoming – my impatience – but I didn't want to expose that as Erin pressed the issue. I preferred to just get into our boat as soon as possible. I thought the beauty of Railay Beach would divert our attention, if we only reached it in time.

Erin and I beheld the ocean in awe. Just as I'd hoped, we were distracted by the shoreline that grew in size and splendor as our enlarged perspective enabled us to see more of the coastline's rocks, towering trees, and white sands. It felt like we had been standing inches away from a massive painting before slowly stepping backward from the canvas, finally allowed to regard the masterpiece from a proper vantage point. Soon, we rounded a looming, 80-foot rock structure guarding Railay's beach from the ocean's open waves. I thought we had left our spat behind us. Erin hadn't brought up our disagreement, and we were both loving the sunshine and saltwater.

A short boat ride couldn't wash away a deeply-entrenched internal issue, however. The decision to not ride our scooter hadn't produced my sharp edge that morning. I had longed for some type of daring adventure throughout our last two weeks, and I felt I wasn't getting what I wanted. More precisely, I felt Erin was holding me back.

Our boat's hull slid onto the sand and we jumped into the shallows. As I tilted my head to look at nature's skyscraper rising overhead, it was as if the sand locked my ankles in place. The sheer size of the rock formations was breathtaking. While I've done my fair share of traveling, I'd never seen such stunning tropics. I'd fallen into the trance that enchants every little kid who walks into Disney World for the first time. They stop in place, astounded by the magic surrounding them.

"Look, E, that's amazing!" I pointed 70 feet above us to a group of climbers ascending one of the rock formations. They were high enough that I could cover them with my one of my thumbs. They had clearly hiked through the rainforest to access their climbing route, which only increased my desire to give it a shot.

I tried fishing for permission while I stood in the shallows, "So, that'd be cool if I could get a guide and go climb too... right?"

"Uh, sure. We can definitely do that another time. We could have done it this time, but we didn't plan it," Erin replied coldly, watching the ant-like climbers. She knew where I was going.

"So, wha..." I trailed off.

I knew she was right. I hadn't planned to climb before we arrived at the beach. I couldn't justify saying, "Surprise! I'm going to climb by myself during the last days of our honeymoon, bye!" It didn't change the fact that I still wanted to go, however.

———

One hour later, I switched tactics, "So, what do we do now?"

It was childish, but I figured that if I framed the question with a, "Is there actually anything interesting to do here?" angle, I might be released from the boredom of sitting on the beach. Erin, however, just wanted to spend quality time relaxing together. Like I had promised we'd do. She likes to talk, and she especially likes to talk with me, so my wanderlust was thwarting her idea of an ideal day at the beach.

I gave up my not-so-subtle campaign and committed to lying on the beach. I decided to first run into the waves and swim out to sea as fast as I could muster, figuring that the more I tired myself out, the longer I'd sit still. Once my arms felt heavy, I looked back to the shoreline and saw Erin with her proverbial "hands on her hips." She was not thrilled to see me swimming through the same waters that long-tail boats cruised with exposed propellers.

"Great," I thought to myself, "I can't even go swimming."

I slowly floated back to shore, not wanting to return too quickly. As I planted myself on the beach a few yards from Erin's home base, I noticed a handful of dwarf crabs skittering across the sand. I dug my hands into the grit to figure out where they were coming from. As I sat quietly, I realized there were scores of crabs standing out against the sand's white backdrop. They retreated into their sand-holes as soon as someone approached. I occupied myself for a few minutes before crawling back to Erin.

"Did you see the crabs? They're pretty cool. Want to go in the water now?" I asked hopefully.

"Can you just hang here for a little bit?"

"On the beach?" I had heard what she said – I just wanted her to reconsider her request.

"Yeah, right here. I just want to spend time with you, Nate."

"Oh, okay."

Within a few minutes, I tried fishing again, "What about kayaks? That guy's renting out two-person kayaks. It could be an us-thing. Yeah?"

"Nate, I don't want to kayak. I just want to stay here with you for a little bit. Okay?"

I rolled my eyes again, "Yeah, fine. Let's do that."

"When you're ready to talk, let's talk, because I'm not enjoying this," Erin retorted.

She was right. It was time for us to talk. I was bottled-up and the longer I stayed that way, the more pressure I'd unleash during an inevitable meltdown.

My first step was to justify my attitude. "I feel like I've been on a leash during the whole trip. In each city, we've tailored how we travel, where we travel, and what we do to what you're comfortable with. I just want a day where you trust me enough to step out of what's familiar and come on an adventure. That's all. I just want one big adventure."

"Isn't this whole trip our adventure? Isn't our marriage the adventure? We went to the national park, you took us to that other beach and climbed the rocks – are you saying those things weren't fun for you?" Erin asked, incredulously.

"Yeah, it is, and yeah, those things were fun. But they were all ratcheted down like 15 levels, you know? Sure, we did go to the national park, but we left after we lost the trail and you got nervous. Then you freaked out at the other beach while I was climbing the ledge and the ocean sprayed me. We were there, but I couldn't enjoy it because I had to cater to you."

I paused for a brief moment before continuing, "And I'd love to go off and do stuff on my own sometimes, but I also know you love our time together – sometimes more than me. So, I just feel guilty whenever I do get time to adventure off."

"It's killing the little fire inside me. That's how I feel, at least," I added.

Can you guess where this is headed?

Tears.

Erin could only respond with tears at first. She wasn't angry; she was just confused. While I knew she wouldn't enjoy what I had to say, I thought I had achieved a nice balance of candor and gentleness. I also knew I wasn't wholly in the right, and that Erin's feelings mattered just as much – if not more – than my wants, so I had offered that as a consideration, too. However, and very understandably, Erin wasn't interested in learning that her husband's "fire" had been reduced to a faint glow. Especially not on her honeymoon.

I watched her tears mix with the sand. I thought about how tears and oceanwater both have salt in them. We talked for a while longer and Erin expressed how she felt. I acquiesced that I should have communicated better (with less eye-rolling), and I confessed that I could have allayed my concerns by simply sharing how I felt earlier in the trip.

Afterward, I laid silently by Erin's side with my head resting on the sweltering sand. I listened to the soft hiss of the sand boiling in the Thai sun. I started to see that Erin hadn't wanted to prevent me from new experiences – it was actually quite the opposite. She was excited by the idea of a brave new adventure with her husband. She just wanted to make decisions together, as a team.

Yet, there I was, splitting my attention. I was focused on myself while also attempting to grow our relationship through quality time. I failed in both regards, and I fumbled my way into the realization that we can't have it both ways. I couldn't retain my former, single freedoms while also expecting to cultivate a full marriage. To gain something – love and a fulfilling life with my wife – I had to sacrifice something – my old autonomy.

———

It struck me somewhere over the Pacific Ocean as we flew home. God hadn't called me to give up my adventurous spirit – my "Nateness," if you will – in marriage. Rather, he called me to infuse what makes me "me" into life with Erin. He was showing me that our relationship works best when I focus my proclivity to wander on writing a new story together, as husband and wife.

Just like Walter Hobbs choosing to search for Buddy the Elf and discovering profound joy in reconnecting with his family, I too was faced with a choice. Choosing to prioritize Erin's needs over my wants was a measuring stick for the growth I had (or hadn't) made in our story. My choice (or lack thereof) was a turning point. It imparted a critical lesson upon me; whenever I believe the world's story was written in service to my desires, narcissism has blinded me to the reality that through sacrifice, I stand to gain far greater meaning. When I'm asked to give up my plans, it's because our Creator is writing a story I wouldn't want to miss. It's backward, but that's how life in the Big Story works.

Some of the greatest minds of our time understood this very well. In fact, CS Lewis argued that we often fail to release our desires simply because we can't see the bigger picture. We can't imagine that forgoing our ambition will result in something of greater value. He outlines this in *The Weight of Glory* by writing:

> It would seem that Our Lord finds our desires not too strong, but too weak. We are half-hearted creatures, fooling about with drink and ambition when infinite joy is offered us, like an ignorant child who wants to go on making mud pies in a slum because he cannot imagine what is meant by the offer of a holiday at the sea. We are far too easily pleased.[xxii]

While Our Lord offered me meaningful connection and adventure alongside my wife, I was focused on building my own sandcastles on Railay Beach. Had I relinquished my selfish focus, I'd have realized what I stood to gain, and I'd have avoided bringing my wife to tears. I guess this is just one of those lessons I'll always need to come back to. From bunk beds to beaches, to infinity and beyond.

———

"Hey, want to rent that two-person kayak?" Erin smiled, studying my expression. "I bet we could paddle out and around the bend."

"That sounds amazing!" I exclaimed, pulling Erin to her feet.

We did rent that kayak, and it was a blast. After we paddled beyond the end of Railay Beach, I slid out of our boat and swam to a small reef. It was brimming with brightly scaled fish. I floated with the lively marine life riding the waves like rollercoasters. I unclipped a waterproof case hanging from my life jacket and I took a picture of Erin paddling around. I still look at that photo whenever I need a reminder that Erin and I are a team, and I've gained one amazing wife through the best choice I've ever made.

Do you remember the last life-defining choice you were asked to make? Are you being asked to make a hard choice in this season of your life? It may be hard to grasp it now if sacrifice is involved, but do you see what you stand to gain in the process?

Fishing 101

June 2017

- complex life lessons come in simple packages -

*It was such a modest and unassuming craft, but as I looked into
the water, I realized just how many profound life lessons
were wrapped up in that fishing net.*

———————

Writing a truly satisfying ending to a story is a fine art.
We know that all stories must come to an end, so we
carry certain expectations for *how* the story ends. We get upset
if the final act doesn't follow a set of universal, conventional
rules, or contain the normal elements we expect. We feel
disenchanted at best and cheated at worst.

A proper ending, of course, must bring decisive and certain
resolution to the story's conflict. If the story cuts out as
Cinderella is on her way to the ball or as Michael J. Fox fires up
his 1980 DeLorean, we cry out injustice. There can't be any loose
ends left unaddressed or we'll find ourselves roaming the empty

hallways of our homes at 2 a.m., distraught and debating how the story should have ended. Well, that would be extreme, but I'm sure it's happened in the history of stories.

A satisfying finale also revisits the core themes introduced to us in the beginning. To realize how far the story has taken us, we want to see where we've been. Lessons, characters, quotes, or flashbacks from earlier chapters are usually woven into the finish line to ensure the ending is well-done. In the same way, we want to feel empathy for the main characters at the end, which only happens if we see evidence they've matured since the start of the story. Did they finally learn their lesson(s)?

———

I didn't have to wait long for my next adventure. The very next day – our last day in Thailand – Erin and I decided to take our scooter to a beach called Ao Nang. Ao Nang has a mile-long, stone-paved strip of shops and restaurants near the water. We figured we'd relish the last hours of our honeymoon by hanging out on the beach in the morning, and then strolling down the strip to find mango sticky rice before heading to the airport.

We parked our scooter at the end of the strip and walked to the furthest end of the beach. We were about a mile away from the strip's busyness by the time we stopped at a massive wall of rocks. Tropical plants, leaves, and green brush grew up the face of the rock wall, creating a perfect habitat for wild monkeys who scurried from branch to branch.

There weren't many distractions around us, which was great. I was committed to staying put on the beach this time. I wanted us to recall a final day of sweet memories after our last conversation about balancing my need for adventure with Erin's expectations of spending time relaxing together.

By now, it shouldn't surprise you to learn that after 30 minutes of hanging out on our beach towels, I was restless. I wanted to move and explore. I guess the feeling that I was losing time spurred me forward. I wanted to maximize my final hours.

I was on the lookout for something new, so when I saw a group of three guys dragging a net through chest-high water, I pointed them out to Erin. "Hey, check it out. It looks like they're missing one guy, right? Like there should be four of them out there?"

Two men stood next to each other and the third stood ten yards away, straining to stay above the water and really leaning into the tide. Waves broke over the trio's heads as nearby long-tail boats pushed rolling waves towards them. It looked like one of those old arcade games where a sweeping arm pushes tokens over a ledge.

As we observed them from afar, we noticed a black line bobbing above the surface. It was their fishing net, which ran from the top of the water down to the ocean floor. They worked the net as a team, trapping small fish that could be sold at the local market. One of the men operated his end solo, struggling to keep command of the net as the waves surged. It would rise too high as the waves swelled, allowing fish to escape underneath.

After the man lost his footing and fell face-first into the sky-blue water, I remarked to Erin, "I think that guy needs my help."

I winced, realizing I had reverted back to prioritizing my idea of fun over Erin's. I studied her for a few more seconds, gauging her reaction before changing my comment to a question. "Do you think I should help him?"

"Do I think you should? Sure, if you want to. So long as I can hang out here, you go for it." Erin set me free, put her sunglasses on, and settled back onto her towel.

I ran down to the waterline and dove into the swell, pulling myself through the rise and fall of the waves. The ocean floor sloped along a shallow gradient, which meant I had to swim 50 yards before approaching the fishermen standing in chest-high water. As I drew closer, I saw how the operation was supposed to work. One guy commanded the top of the net and sat higher in the water, while the other worked the bottom and sat lower.

I swam up to the man who was working alone. He was holding the right side of the net flush to the ocean floor with his feet, while wrapping the top of the net around his hands to stretch the trap to its full length. This setup made it awkward for him to walk, let alone battle the undulating waves.

I soon learned his nickname was Whiskey (for what reason, I can only guess), so I asked, "Hey Whiskey, can I help you?"

He nodded, signaling he understood, despite not speaking much English. He unraveled the upper rope from his palms and held it out for me to take, which I did. While it may sound like he relinquished a simple and straightforward job, as soon as I took the rope, it was clear I was an amateur. I lacked the local's touch. Whiskey moved my hands up and down as I dropped them too low, or brought them too high, based on the ocean's movement. He didn't say anything; he just moved my hands into position until I got the right idea.

One of the guys across the net shouted to me, "Name? Name?!"

"Name? Oh, my name's Nate!" I yelled back, looking down to make sure I wasn't mishandling the net.

"Net! Ah! Yes! Good!" He chuckled, clearly amused that my English name sounded like the instrument we were dragging through the sea.

"You no fish good," the other one yelled, laughing.

Whiskey reminded me to wait for the tide to surge before pulling the net toward shore, which would leverage the ocean's force and save my strength. I think the trio found my lack of fishing skill especially hilarious because they believed my parents had named me "Net." I was okay with that. I was clearly the new kid on the block.

We landed the net after a few more minutes of battling the waves and we dragged the black ropes away from the ocean's prying fingers, which threatened to claw back our catch if we weren't careful.

"Oh yes, big fish. Good. Good!" Leo, the fellow who had first asked me my name, said as he picked up a six-inch fish between three fingers.

I look down at my wrinkly, ocean-soaked fingers before looking back to Leo's, which held the fish. Despite laboring in the water for hours, Leo's hands didn't appear pruney. I guess they were just battle-worn, accustomed to the endless sun and saltwater. That felt right to me. He was clearly the leader of the group. He'd probably spent the better part of his adult life in the water. As Leo continued inspecting our catch, he yelled to a group of women sitting on wicker baskets. Then, he paced the length of the outstretched net and showed me which fish were good to keep and which we should throw back into the water.

As we separated the sour tasting, spiny, and poisonous fish from the ones that could be sold in the market, Leo pointed at my wedding ring. "Wife?" he asked.

"Yes, that's her," I pointed toward Erin, lying on the beach about 40 yards away.

"Oh yes. Good! I have family," Leo said, spreading a big smile across his tanned face and pointing to his own wedding ring.

The women collected the remaining fish writhing on the sand as we gathered our net to haul it back into the water for another round. We waded into the ocean in unison, moving as one even line and lifting the net above the water until we were in deeper territory. As we pushed out from shore, I asked Whiskey, Leo, and Tiger – the third guy's nickname – questions about fishing, their life in Thailand, and how they met each other.

I had to rely on their broken English to communicate since I didn't speak a lick of Thai (I regularly confused "good morning" with "thank you" throughout the trip). As we strode into the sea, I began to understand more of their respective stories. Whiskey was 16 years old, and he had left school to fish and make money. Tiger fished because he liked the water and it was his father's trade. Leo had a family to provide for, and his wife bundled the fish for sale at the local market so it was a family business.

I pointed to the high noon sun to ask how long they would work that day. Leo traced his finger from straight up in the sky, signaling daytime, down into the water, representing the sun disappearing below the horizon. It was going to be a long day.

Although I was in decent shape, fishing with a hand-net was intense. I felt completely spent after just 45 minutes of hauling that net through the surf. Although Whiskey and I rotated from the right to the left side of the net to switch up the muscles we used, I could tell I would be sore the following morning.

I gestured to Whiskey, rubbing my thumb against two fingers to create the universal sign for money. "Will it be a good day?"

He nodded, holding up 10 fingers to show his estimate. He was translating his income into dollars for me. $10 USD would be his take. For context, between our Airbnb, eating out, and Thai massages, Erin and I easily spent $100 USD that day. In other words, I'd have to haul fishing nets for 10 full days to afford one day of our vacation (let alone the airfare to fly there).

I took my turn managing the bottom of the net after a few more rounds of landing our catch and wading back out to sea. As I ducked below a wave that crashed overhead with blue and white foam, I realized that every mistake I made, raising our net too high or closing it in too narrowly, was ultimately costing the trio a small amount of income. Yet, despite my lack of fishing skill, they seemed to genuinely enjoy having a white guy around.

It was such a modest and unassuming craft, but as I looked into the water, I realized just how many profound life lessons were wrapped up in that fishing net. Countless thoughts swam through my mind, all arising from such a humble source.

Our fishing net reminded me of a proverb that says, "If you want to go fast, go alone. If you want to go far, go together." With some practice, I could have dragged a smaller net through the water by tying the ends to both my hands and feet. Working as a team was taking us further, however. Four people created an increasing return for our labor as were able to maneuver a net with a surface area much larger than just four times the size of a single person's net. Ultimately, that meant the trio were more than co-workers. They depended on each other. Without their team, they might not provide enough income for their families.

Putting that in the context of Erin and myself, I wondered, "Could Erin and I survive off 10 bucks a day?" I debated if we could go without the nice things of life. You know, coconut ice cream, ski trips, wild-caught instead of farm-raised salmon, that kind of stuff. I decided we'd always stay together, even if we had to give up the luxury around us. I knew that was the case before fishing of course, but it sank in as I thought about us as a team, not separate people who simply love and live with each other.

To a fault, I like to figure things out on my own. In the little and big things alike, I only feel worthy if I can solve challenges, build things, and fix problems through my own wit. For years I had cultivated a self-sufficient mentality, and foolishly, I had brought that mindset into my marriage. It reared its ugly head on our honeymoon, and I felt guilty as I realized that the idea I would depend on someone so closely – just like Whiskey, Tiger, and Leo did for their income – was totally foreign to me.

I looked across the waves to Erin lying on her towel. While most people would have labeled me as serving, supportive, or sacrificing, in reality, too many of my model-husband actions rose up from a deep well of pride that pushed me to do more and be more. I wanted to be the hero who provided. I didn't want to accept help for myself. Drinking from that same well of self-sufficiency, I had tried to live my own Thai adventure instead of making joint decisions as a team; exactly what operating a four-person fishing net was teaching me to do.

Whiskey hollered and snapped my attention back to the net. It was being lifted by the swell like a parachute. I remembered my place on the team and re-focused.

―――――

"Man, I feel like I should pay these guys!" I exclaimed, sprinting up the beach to Erin. The riptides had pushed us a few hundred yards down the shoreline so I was out of breath and talking excitedly.

"You know, people pay a lot of money for 'local' experiences while they're on vacation. Like cooking classes and stuff. I just lucked out and got that one for free. I think they should start charging for this, maybe package it with a fish dinner. I could help them figure out the business model."

Erin chuckled, "Nate, you realize you're probably the only one on this beach who wants to handle spiky fish and drag nets through the water?"

"What? No way. I don't think so. There was a whole group of tourists taking pictures and watching us haul the last net. They were jealous."

"Or maybe they were wondering why you were doing manual labor on vacation," she teased, standing from the sand and shaking out her towel.

"Yeah, maybe. I learned a lot though. There's more to fishing than you'd think." We started our walk back to Ao Nang's main strip as I explained my thoughts.

"Why don't we buy them beer? That lady's selling some over there." I leaned against Erin's shoulder to divert her path toward a Thai lady sitting on a white cooler in a large sunhat. She was holding up beer and pineapples.

"Oh, let's get some pineapple, too. Those skewers are delicious," Erin said, closing her eyes to remember the sweet taste of grilled fruit.

"Whatever you'd like." I took her hand in mine and slipped her backpack over my shoulder. "You know I love you, right?"

"I do. But thanks for saying it anyway," Erin smiled as she leaned on my shoulder.

All Stories Must Have Endings

- your life story isn't actually about you -

Of course, we'll accept a lesser role in a bigger story because it will be immensely more fulfilling than living at the center of a lesser story.

Y ou'd be hard pressed to find someone who doesn't have at least one social media account. We're all on Facebook, Instagram, LinkedIn, and other social sites to keep connected. These platforms do help us connect, but more importantly, they allow us to create – or rather curate – a profile that projects a certain narrative about who we are, where we've been, and where we're going. Social profiles enable us to control what others believe about us by deploying pictures, events, and posts that formulate our preferred storyline.

This profile-driven approach to relating with the world puts us in charge of writing our own stories, every single day. When we combine this capacity with a very post-truth culture, which tells us that truth is what we'd like it to be, and feelings matter more than facts, it's easy to lose sight of the reality that our life stories aren't actually about us. "Seek and find *your* truth" we're told today. But this is where our blindness begins.

We all crave to live a meaningful life. Selfishly, we want to be the hero of the story. If there is no absolute truth and everything in life is relative, or based upon personal preference, then we are indeed free to direct our lives as we please. There's no sovereign authority to which we need to answer. With no sovereign presence, we become the driving force behind our own life's meaning. Social media further places us in the driver's seat as we spin photos and status updates into feelings of significance, or stories for others to admire. Effectively, a post-truth culture presented through social media gives me the ability to live at the center of my own little world.

For every ten people to whom I describe this idea – that we're not the center of our life stories, our Creator is, and that we're just characters in the Big Story of our world – I see eight blank stares in return. One person usually says, "That's interesting, tell me more." Another will say, "I know! How cool is that?!" This belief that we're not the center of our lives, and that we don't have complete control over them, is not a popular one.

It feels "un-American" to tell someone they're not wholly self-made. It's "narrow-minded" to believe our worth is rooted in a single, supreme creator – an author.

Yet far too often, we wander through life in search of identity and significance when infinite worth and eternal meaning is already offered to us. If we'd simply accept that we're all characters passing through a fraction of a story that's been ongoing for thousands of years before us, we'd find greater meaning. Even during our ordinary days.

Here's another way to think about this. If you were given the choice of being an all-star pitcher for your 3rd grade baseball team, or a sub-par relief pitcher for the Chicago Cubs during the 2016 World Series, which would you choose? That should be a no-brainer. Of course, we'll accept our slot as a mediocre relief pitcher (a lesser role in a bigger story) because it's immensely more fulfilling than living at the center of a lesser story.

Yet, we ignore this reality when we live as the focal point of our individual stories, instead of living as part of the Big Story. We want to be the hero. We don't want to admit we're just humble characters. And that's the Gospel story in a nutshell – God loves us, so He gives us a role in His story, despite all the times we flip the script and believe we're in control. He even created a path through grace to be with Him at the end of the story. Do you know of any other stories that end with both the characters and their author actually meeting, face-to-face?

———

At the end of it all, if we accept we're not authors, only characters, and that meaning often shows up in ways that feel backward to us, we will uncover greater purpose and joy for our ordinary days. We'll find undying, permanent fulfillment when we're no longer scrambling to determine the direction of our lives or construct our own significance.

Moreover, when we give up the need to control our stories, we can know how our story ends. We don't have to wait. The Author of Life has already let us in on the mystery through His written word, the Bible.

I used to believe the Bible was just a series of isolated, separate historical stories with wise sayings for good living. Then I discovered that each chapter builds on the prior, leading up to one magnificent crescendo of an ending when the hero, God's Son, Jesus, returns to Earth.

It's a story written like no other. Its entirety is unified by a single plotline. A single strand of truth was woven throughout 66 books, written over 2,000 years, by 40 different authors, writing on three continents, in three different languages, all from separate life experiences.

Consider the gravity of that for a moment. Absent a divine creator orchestrating it all, how is it possible that this amount of diversity produced such a unified, integrated storyline?

Now, as we find ourselves at the end of my story, consider

your own for a moment. Do you see the possibility of a bigger storyline unfolding around you?

Do you feel you're living a story that has ultimate meaning? Ultimate purpose?

Does your story have the "big" kind of joy? The joy that transcends setbacks and rainy seasons?

Could living in light of our Author's Big Story change your answer(s)?

One Last Thing

If you've enjoyed reading this book, and think that others might also enjoy reading it, could you help me out by doing one (or more) of the following things?

1. Leave a review on Amazon.com letting others know why you enjoyed this book.
2. Post a picture of your copy of this book on Facebook, Instagram, Twitter, or any other social platform.
3. Sign up for my email list at www.livefwd.org to keep up-to-date on new stories, releases, and giveaways.

Also, I'll make you a deal. If you suggest this book to a friend and they don't feel it was worth their time, I'll pay for them to go see a movie instead.

Really, I will. They can email nate@livefwd.org and say, "Nate, I just read your book and wish I had that time back. I want to go see a movie, here's my PayPal/ Venmo/ QuickPay email."

Acknowledgements

To the many people I have and haven't mentioned in this book, each of you have played an enormously influential and defining role in my life's story. Thank you, so very much.

To Phil, my brother & best bud – Thank you for being someone who I look up to and model myself after, even if I may have called you 'Little Man' for the first 18 years of your life. Thank you for seeking adventures, for being your own person, and for writing your own story. I, like many others in your life, admire who you are and who God's shaping you to be.

To Rachael – Thank you sharpening and cementing within me a never-fading, never-dulling perseverance and belief that I can do anything. Thank you for encouraging me in my life's pursuits and thank you for marrying an equally awesome man in Luke. **Luke**, I'm so glad we're now a part of each other's story.

To Rebekah – Thank you for showing me how beautiful gentleness and compassion can be. Thank you for helping me understand it's okay to do the things you like just because you like them. I'm thrilled to see the story you're writing, and I'm thankful that our bond will always transcend cities and states.

To Mom & Dad – Thank you for making every one of my adventures and life lessons possible, for believing in me, and enabling me to do what gives me life. Above all, thank you for pointing me to the joy of living my life in light of our Creator.

To Daniel – Thank you for sharing 20+ years of my life and for writing hundreds of my life's most formative stories with me. Thank you for always having the brightest smile and the loudest laugh in the room, and for sharing your early morning coffee and late evening tea with me for years. Also, thank you to **the whole Kuppler family** for loving me, accepting me, and for giving me a second home to grow up in.

To Ryan D. – Thank you for knowing the encouragement that I need before I say any words, and for showing me what it looks like to walk calmly and confidently. I'll always be in your corner, watching and cheering as the Lord unfolds his plan for your life.

To Brian – Thank you for teaching me to trust myself, to go with my gut, to be genuine, and to ask why people say and think what they do. Thank you for being the example of how, when we commit to ceaseless action and service, we can make our corner of the world a better place. Our world needs more of you in it.

To Greg – Thank you for showing me what consistency and authenticity looks like, for being "Greg" in every setting, and for having the emotional capacity to share in my deepest joys and saddest sorrows alike. I'll always keep a futon in your honor.

To David – Thank you for never taking anything at face value, for always being your own person, and for modeling what sacrificial love should look like. I can honestly say, beyond a shadow of a doubt, that I know you would be at my side anytime I needed it. I love you for it, and I would do the same.

To Kyle – Thank you for reading the early version of this book when it was nothing more than ramblings and run-on sentences, and for offering your perceptive and candid point-of-view to help me shape the narrative. More so, thank you for shaping my life in and after college, just like an older brother.

To Mo – Thank you for being an unwavering and committed man of the Lord, for sharing your wisdom and direction from one life stage ahead of me to another, and for pointing me back to scripture during my questions and doubts.

To Ryan O. – Thank for caring about me more than your own comfort, for seasoning your words with grace and through them, shaping how I now relate to, speak with, and uplift others. Finally, thank you for packing more joy and laughter than I thought was possible into each of your shoulder-shaking jokes.

To Sam – Thank you for your quiet faithfulness, for displaying resilience during the lows of a life's story, for showing humility during the highs, and for your steadfast friendship. No matter what city I live in, there'll always be a food-crawl to be had when you're in town.

To Jeff – Thank you for showing me how to work diligently and how to pursue a career without losing sight of life's important things. Thank you for living with curiosity, for offering me meaningful conversation when I need it most, for being a part of my story during its most formative years, and for being the world's most-interesting-man-undercover.

To JJ – Never have I met someone who brings the character and love of Jesus Christ out of history and into life like you. Thank you for showing me what it looks like to love people, regardless of their story, and for keeping me company with questions and conversation during every road trip I've ever taken since college.

To Ryan & Kristen – Thank you for welcoming me into your lives and family with open arms, for supporting Erin and I throughout all chapters of our story, and for backing us with a love that far exceeds what in-laws and families are called to give.

To Kathy – It takes an amazing mother to raise an amazing daughter, and I'm so grateful that Erin's had – and always will have – you to love her. I smile when I see moments of firm resolve and tender squeals of delight alike welling up inside Erin because I know that is you shining through her personality.

To Tiffany – Thank you for always being on Team Nate, for being smarter than everyone else in the room, for being so easily lovable, and for being a loyal and steady friend and roommate – not only to Erin, but to me as well.

References

[i] Chesterton, G. K. *Orthodoxy*. United States: Popular Classics Publishing, 2012.

[ii] Lewis, C. S. *The Weight of Glory: And Other Addresses*. San Francisco: HarperSanFrancisco, 2005.

[iii] Helveston, Jason C. "Rest." Blog - Jason C. Helveston. August 1, 2017. www.jasonhelveston.com/blog/2017/8/1/rest.

[iv] Lewis, C. S. *Mere Christianity*. Enfield, N.S.W.: Royal Blind Society, 1957.

[v] Godin, Seth. "Light on Your Feet." Seth's Blog. December 11, 2015. www.sethgodin.typepad.com/seths_blog/2015/12/light-on-your-feet.html.

[vi] *Matthew 11:29*. In *Holy Bible NIV*. Grand Rapids, MI: Zondervan, 2011.

[vii] Chesterton, G. K. Heretics. London: John Lane, 1919.

[viii] Rittenhouse, Nathan. "The Problem of Proximity." RZIM. February 8, 2018. www.rzim.org/a-slice-of-infinity/problem-of-proximity/.

[ix] Joshua 4. In Holy Bible CEV. Grand Rapids, MI: Zondervan, 2011.

[x] Ibid.

[xi] Tony Robbins Live. By Tony Robbins.

xii Guinness, Os. *The Call: Finding & Fulfilling the Central Purpose of Your Life.* Nashville, TN: Thomas Nelson, 2003.

xiii Miller, Donald. *Scary Close: Dropping the Act and Finding True Intimacy.* Nashville, TN: Nelson Books, 2015.

xiv Trueblood, Elton. *The New Man for Our Time.* New York, NY: Harper Collins, 1970.

xv Lewis, C. S. *Mere Christianity.* Enfield, N.S.W.: Royal Blind Society, 1957.

xvi Lewis, C. S. The Weight of Glory: And Other Addresses. San Francisco: HarperSanFrancisco, 2005.

xvii Zacharias, Ravi. "Let My People Think." RZIM. 2017.

xviii "Transcript: Tom Brady, Part 3." Interview. 60 Minutes, November 4, 2005. www.cbsnews.com/news/transcript-tom-brady-part-3/.

xix Philippians 4:11-13. In Holy Bible NIV. Grand Rapids, MI: Zondervan, 2011.

xx Lewis, C. S. Mere Christianity. Enfield, N.S.W.: Royal Blind Society, 1957.

xxi Elf. Directed by Jon Favreau. Performed by Will Ferrell and James Caan. New Line Cinema, 2003. Transcript. November 7, 2003.

xxii Lewis, C. S. The Weight of Glory: And Other Addresses. San Francisco: HarperSanFrancisco, 2005.

Made in the USA
Middletown, DE
23 August 2018